THE LOST YOU

THE JOURNEY CALLED LIFE

Rajeev Dua

Rajeev Dua 2021

All rights reserved.
ISBN: 978-978-985-180-5

The right of Rajeev Dua to be identified as the Author
of this Work has been asserted by him in accordance with the
Nigerian Copyright Act.

Edited by Eze Nkoyo Onyekachukwu

No part of this publication may be reproduced, stored in a retrieval
system, or transmitted, in any form or by any means, without the
prior permission in writing of the Author or publisher, nor be
otherwise circulated in any form of binding or cover other than that
in which it is published and without a similar condition including
this condition being imposed on the subsequent purchaser.

A CTC catalogue record of this book is available from the
National Library, Lagos, Nigeria.

First Edition

णमो अरिहंताणं
णमो सिद्धाणं
णमो आयरियाणं
णमो उवज्झायाणं
णमो लोएसव्वसाहूणं

एसो पंच णमोयारो,
सव्व पावप्पणासणो।

मंगलाणं च सव्वेसिं
पढमं हवई मंगलम् ।।

Blessings in Hindi from my Mentor

Contents

Contents

Acknowledgment

I would like to thank Nigeria (Lagos) for providing me with the right environment and mindset that helped me write this book, though the thought of writing this book was in me for almost five years.

Dr. Harbhajan Singh Batth played a key role in encouraging and motivating me to pen down my thoughts in the form of this book.

I would also like to thank Mr. Matthew, my dear friend and local guardian in Lagos, for patiently listening to my thoughts and encouraging me to write.

This book would not have seen the light of the day without the unconditional support of my dear friend, Mrs. Suziette Agazie (Sush). She helped me organize my thoughts into this form. Just saying 'thanks' to you will not be sufficient to appreciate your contributions to this book.

Last but not the least, I would like to thank my family and friends - my son Aryan, my wife Charu, my father Mr. J. L. Dua, my mother late Mrs. Jyoti Dua, my brother Sanjeev and friends Kamal, Ravi, Suresh, Raghav and Prashant (Lagos) for being with me as a pillar throughout my life.

My wholehearted respect to my mentor, my Guruji; Balacharya Shri 108 Siddhasen Ji Maharaj, for his love and blessings.

The Journey Called Life

When I was born, I was a little dark but more towards brown.
Yet, my parents made me wear an invisible crown

I was happy with my childhood habit.
But my life made me run like a rabbit

My life was going very happy
But I forget my parents who helped me changed my nappy

When I grew up in my life
I was blessed with a wonderful kid and a beautiful wife

I was running with my honey, to earn a lot of money
In the process, I lost my peace and harmony

I made houses, farms, offices and made a lot of wealth
Somewhere in this race, I compromised with my own health

I wish to relive those old golden days
But I know, I've lost them in some old dark bays

My friend, it's still not too late
Pick up the pen and paper and rewrite your own fate

You should leave behind that artificial you
The sky that side is still clear and blue

You will once again see birds chirping in the bright sky
Remove that invisible lair from you and bid him goodbye

"Find yourself before it is too late."

ज़िंदगी का कारवां

ज़िंदगी का कारवां आगे बढ़ता गया, और मैं बाबू से बेबी, बेबी से हनी और हनी से डैडी बनता गया !
मगर इस सफर मे जाने कहीं मैं अपना बचपन खोता गया !!

ज़िंदगी का कारवां आगे बढ़ता गया, नाम के आगे मास्टर, मिस्टर, डॉक्टर, डिअर, रेस्पेक्टेड और ऑनरेबल लगता गया !
मगर इस सफर मे जाने कहीं मैं अपना वजूद खोता गया !!

ज़िंदगी का कारवां आगे बढ़ता गया, और मैं खूब ज्ञान अर्जित करता गया !
मगर इस सफर मे जाने कहीं बस मैं अपनी आत्मा को विसर्जित करता गया !!

ज़िंदगी का कारवां आगे बढ़ता गया, नए मकान बनते गए और नए मुकाम मिलते गए !
मगर इस सफर मे जाने कहीं मैं अपना स्वयं का रास्ता भटकता गया !!

ज़िंदगी तुम तो आगे बढ़ गयी, हाँ तुम तो आगे बढ़ गयी !
शायद मैं ही कहीं पीछे छूट गया !!

ऐ सुन,अब भी वक़्त है,याद कर अपनी बुनियाद को,
और उसी बुनियाद के दम पर,तू संभआल अपने आप को!
और ज़िन्दगी की इस दौड़ मे, तू भूल ना अपने आप को, तू भूल ना अपने आप को !!

Preface

We invest our entire lives searching for a lot of materialistic things, hoping to achieve our ambitions. We meet many people in our lives; some remain acquaintances, a few become friends from being acquaintances, and some become family from being just friends.

Unknowingly, we get into a never-ending race of trying to be perfect and please everyone around us. We want to look better than others; therefore, we carry an invisible layer over us.

Our life is like a movie wherein we play the role of many characters simultaneously, and all of these characters are different from each other, yet we have to act in such a way that we fit properly into each one. All these characters around us judge us, and we judge them too. In the process of satisfying everyone and hoping to look better, we start losing our own identity.

I will take the example of myself I am a father, a husband, a son, a son-inlaw, a brother-in-law, a brother, a friend, a neighbor, an uncle, a boss, a subordinate, a colleague, a mentor, a mentee, a student, a businessman, a customer, a writer, a player, and a devotee etc etc .... I behave differently in each role because each role is unique, meaningful, and different from the other.

We get so influenced by our surroundings that many of us go to an extent of choosing a profession that is not in line with our strengths and likes. We choose it to fulfill our financial and social needs, and as a result, we lose our core identity.

'There is no harm in living for others but not at the cost of your own life.'

- Rajeev Dua

"Don't try to create many identities for yourself and forget your own" - Rajeev Dua

Chapter 1

Who am I?

Can you imagine? Your identity was born with you!

There was already a basket chosen for you before you were even born, and the day you were born, you were allocated to that designated basket. A child with the name "Andrew or Maria" goes to a "Christian basket" whereas "Imran or Samina" goes to a "Muslim basket". Kids with the name "Gurpreet Singh or Harleen Kaur" goes to a "Sikh basket," whereas "Ram or Sita" goes to a "Hindu basket."

So based on the basket chosen for you, the festivals you celebrate have been decided, your values are formed, and your beliefs are cascaded to you. Your ways of life are downloaded, your upbringing is done and your habits are formed; these all, to a large extent vary and determine who you are. The irony of life is that you did not even have a clue about this.

So here this starts the confusion journey.

When you start growing, you are labeled by your society as whether you resemble your paternal or maternal family and this confusion of your resemblance further deepens and leans towards your identity. In the next stage, your family starts dictating the profession they want for you. Your grandfather starts seeing an engineer in you whereas your grandmother sees a doctor (already assuming that when you grow up, you will take care of her illness).

Also, while your father sees a scientist in you, your mother sees an artist.

So, when you are growing, you are driven, directed, guided and inducted into several streams without even knowing about your own strengths and weaknesses, your likes and dislikes.

Let us go back to the very beginning.

The way you cried your first, the look you gave the medical team or your mother when you were born, the way you fed, the way you slept and how active you were or not, all showed the world your identity. However, as you grew and your identity began to show, you started adapting to the environment you were born into.

As children, we were carefree and our lives were full of fun. We played, ate and slept with school in between; we never understood how our actions and what we perceived all around us would shape who we would be in future. We aspired to be heroes like our favorite movie characters or like our parents. This helped build our confidence and improved our character.

Character builds over time and through activities. As children, we played the role of a dependent. We looked up to our parents, our teachers and the people around us to survive, grow and acquire things. As our characters took form, we metamorphosed into independent people. Then our characters start taking on a personality of their own, and temperaments start to show. This shaped us into the unique human being that we became.

If this unique human being plays so many roles to so many people in so many ways, then who am I truly, and in the process, will I really be able to remember my own identity? Have I not lost myself in being so many characters? Take into cognizance that I change my character, personality and even my temperament as

I grow to satisfy all my roles, looking to perfect them, and as a result will I not have lost my own identity?

It is a question we keep asking ourselves as we grow and it produces different answers every time!

It is funny how you change who you want to be as you grow older. As a child you would have dreamt of being something simple like a teacher or a firefighter, even a nurse, then you grow up, become a teenager and then want to be a rock star or an actor. You want to be fancy and glamorous. Your character becomes flexible to fit your peers, neighborhood, and image your peers have painted for the world to see. Somehow you become focused as you pay attention to what you watch, what you listen to and who you play with.

You see the world from your personal view, a screen you created, and nothing seems impossible or too far to reach. Still sometimes, you feel lost; this is because you might be living a pretentious life, trying to make everyone happy around you.

As a twenty one year old, I was confident of who I was, and I was always trying to prove to people that I knew what I wanted and where I wanted to go. Actually, I did not know. It is a common trait in young adults. Almost every one of us at the early stages of our careers start doing or dreaming based on what we see around us. We get influenced by them and choose our professions due to our surroundings and later get confused with our materialistic achievements and consider them our identity. We feel that this is what we chose when we were growing up, but the reality is that most of us, though we reach our goals and sometimes overachieve our materialistic targets, we lose our core identities in the process/journey. This is due to the influences we allow to guide us out of our own confused state.

I was no different from others, most of my friends from my childhood came from a business background, they used to join family to run their family business after college, due to that influence I also started my job at a very early age. I joined one of the greeting card distributor as an office assistant, later upon my request and interest I was moved to sales function, this stint laid the foundation of my professional journey.

Today, when I look at my family's status, position, wealth, and social image it gives me immense satisfaction that God has been kind to me and given me more than I deserved but somehow I feel that though I might have won this rat race called life, I am still lost to my own-self.

I no longer have time for my family, I no longer have hobbies and I no longer eat with relish just like I used to in the early stage of my life. I no longer like to go for a drive, which used to be my passion. One way or the other, I lost myself.

It is important to play all the roles life has assigned to us judiciously, but at the same time, we should preserve ourselves by keeping that child alive within us. Do not forget your basic likes/dislikes; do not forget the things/acts that give us ultimate pleasure to our soul.

Believe me, friends, one day, this life, without warning, will make you grow, and it will be difficult for you to find yourself. So, it is better that we keep on asking ourselves, "Who am I?" on a regular basis so that we never have to ask this question to ourselves - "Why did I grow up?"

Rather, grow with GRACE.

When I start thinking about my childhood and how free I was, I wonder if one can return to those days. Forget about the worries of the world, what to wear, what to see, what to eat, and so on.

However, these thoughts are never long-lived as I shake myself out of it and concentrate on the life in front of me.

I never thought that I would grow up so fast and forget my youth. They were my most confident and most proactive years. I had fun, parties, friends, and all of life's pleasures. Then one day, without warning, I grew up!

"Your time will never pause, but you can and you should." – Rajeev Dua

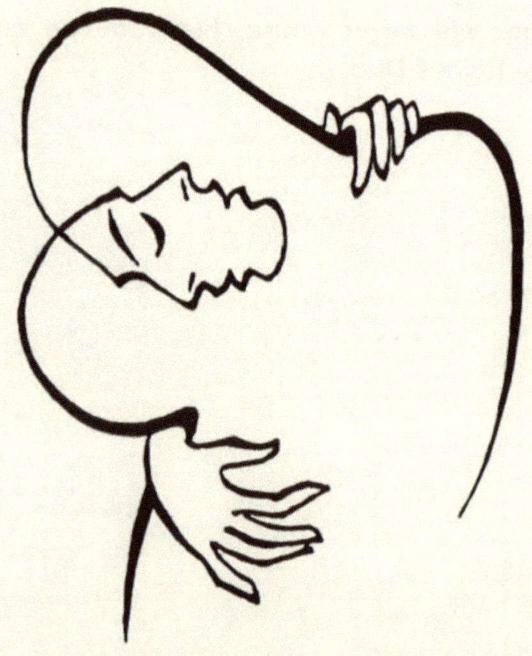

**"You can never show your own back
to yourself" - Rajeev Dua**

Chapter 2

"YOU" are your best friend

First, let us attempt to define a friend. A friend is someone you look up to, that you can rely on, coaches and advises you. Someone you have mutual trust and respect for. A friend will give a shoulder to cry on and will rejoice with you. A friend will accept you as you are without judgment; a friend might even like what you like and dislike what you dislike. Even when he criticizes you, he does so for your own good.

So a friend is someone you know and like very well, someone like you. So why can you not be your own friend?

For you to be a good friend to yourself, you need to know yourself. Hence, the ultimate question is, how well do you know yourself?

Knowing yourself is the first step to being your own friend because you would not make unacquainted people your friends; it is the way to befriend yourself. Now let us look at what it means to know 'yourself.'

Knowing yourself is knowing who you are - your likes, dislikes, strengths, weaknesses, favorite movie, food, places, hobbies, favorite people, etc. It is knowledge of everything you consider good which gives you happiness.

The reason I am bringing this back to your knowledge is that, in the journey called life, we all tend to forget ourselves and seek friendships in the outer world, whereas the best friend is sitting closest to you; your best friend is "You" among all your friends.

People usually make the mistake of picking friends based on their social lives, social status, and their family backgrounds, and this should not be. There is a difference between a friend and an acquaintance. An acquaintance does not know you well nor accepts all you do. Many people mistake acquaintances with friendship. You need to understand the difference and not mistake it.

Back in India, I had so many friends because I am a very social person. I hung out a lot with so many people. I had a fascinating social life. I usually hung out with these people, I termed friends, and on my first trip to Nigeria, I had so many of them call me regularly to check up on me.

When I first moved to Nigeria, I got many calls from these friends. It has been almost two years since I relocated to Nigeria and as I sit, I wonder if most of them were really friends because a lot of them do not call anymore. I am now far away and as the saying goes, out of sight is out of mind. This has changed the perspective of my understanding of people.

I also appreciate that each of our acquaintances have their own challenges/priorities in life and remembering someone in absentia is not easy, this is quite practical. One should not make much of it, it is the way life is; or else it might lead to dissatisfaction.

Friends are there for you through thick and thin, whether you are present or absent. They will fight for you and care for you.

In life, it is a given that people will judge and misinterpret you, it is your friends that will stand up for you and help you through tough times. This is why it is important that you should be your own friend because sometimes, when you are alone, you will have to help yourself through those tough times as no one else is available.

So yes, you need to be your best friend, understand yourself, and advise yourself because no one can know you better.

Have you heard the saying, 'You have to love yourself first before someone else will love you'? This saying is accurate as it evokes confidence or weakness when you love or do not love yourself. It is so easy that it is like a note passed on to others to tell them that I love myself, so if you are coming close, you have to love me too.

To love yourself means to accept who you are despite the mischief that you cannot change. You have to have self-respect, a positive self-image, and an unconditional acceptance of who you are. You have to be your friend and most significantly, your best friend.

You have to be honest with yourself, love yourself, and have fun with yourself. You can do this through meditation and even by talking to yourself. This will make you confident in your skin and feel no remorse whatsoever towards yourself. In return, it helps people understand and appreciate you. It also helps conversations with your inner voice.

What is an inner voice?

Sometimes, we hear people say my inner voice, my soul voice, but what really is an inner voice? Your inner voice is you! This is because you know what you are doing, whether it is good or bad, and know the actions you take. You know whether the action is good or bad or whether it has future consequences, yet you do it despite that knowledge. You must agree that we definitely know if what we are doing is good or bad. We definitely see that it can be harmful to us yet, we still do it.

This is why when discussing it, you tell your friend, 'My inner self warned me yet I did it, or my soul was telling me not to do it yet I did it.'

When I say be your own friend, I do not necessarily mean it to help you tackle your loneliness or heal your loneliness. I mean, it will keep you in check and help you make the right decisions, keeping you on the right track. You must listen to yourself and talk to yourself regularly. You can decide to do it literally or through meditation, whatever suits you. You need to understand that to be a better person, you have to tell yourself you can and do it. You have to be determined, focused and most especially, disciplined. Engage in activities that make you happy and keep you away from stress; remember those activities and spend time with them to know yourself better.

Meditation is a great way to find yourself. Staying in a quiet room with no distractions, listening to your breathing, following the rise and fall of your chest helps you understand your body; during meditation, you are not thinking of anybody; you are feeling your own breath.

You are the sum of everything you have ever seen, heard, eaten, smelled, been told, forgotten, it is all there. Everything around you influences you, and because of that, you should try to stay positive. You might wonder why I added 'forgotten'. It is because we do not truly forget things. They live in our subconscious and it can lead us to be, or do something we are not, or do not want to do. Hence the need to stay positive to combat such negative influence.

If you understand yourself very well, you will be able to manage yourself well. I also appreciate the fact that friends are also important in life - as the saying goes, no man is an island. You need friends to help you through life and also to groom you. However, making yourself your friend is not a bad idea. It is actually a good idea, as knowing you helps bring out the best you and most especially, making you your best friend helps you love yourself and makes it easy for others to love you.

Due to my profession, I got transferred to several cities, sometimes I moved with my family and sometimes alone. The reason I was able to cope with those movements is that I made myself my best friend.

You can live an artificial or superficial life to the world. You can make them believe what you are not, but you cannot hide from yourself. This is why it is good to talk to oneself and make yourself aware of who "You" are. Tell yourself the truth, and you will be fine.

Believe me, when all your acquaintances or worldly friends become busy with their daily routines, there will be only one person standing by you always, and that person is "You".

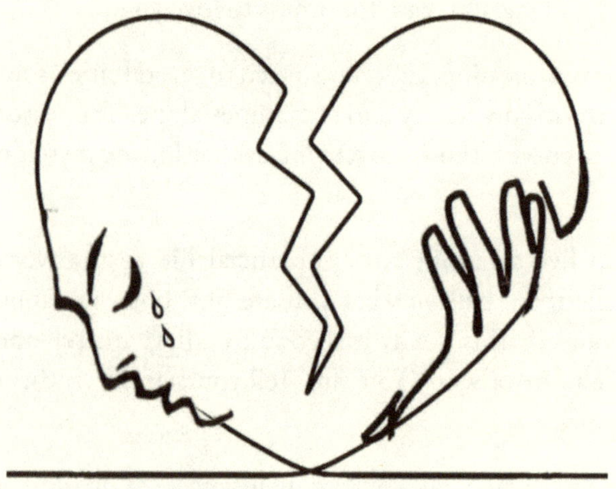

"Attach yet remain detached and detach yet remain attached" – Rajeev Dua

Chapter 3

Attach yet remain detached, detach yet remain attached!

We have been talking about losing our identity while trying to connect with the larger world. Life is basically about attachments. With the present pandemic, people have gone back to their families, their parents and homes. They have gone back to playing cards and video games together, cooking together, and basically strengthening bonds that were stretched or broken due to people's busy schedules.

Now, people are spending quality time with family. Nature has created such an environmental compulsion that people running after materialistic things have stopped, paused, and gone back to what really matters. A lot of us were mostly interested in profit margins, campaigns or talking about sales or business, but now, we are also focusing on family, safety and security, bonding, spending quality time with each other, and spending time with ourselves, looking to be happy. This pandemic has made all of us understand the importance of our families. No-one knows which will be the last day of life. Therefore it is essential that we live and enjoy our lives today rather than having plans to live it tomorrow. Most of us plan: to live tomorrow on today's cost due to the responsibilities. We focus more on the future and postpone living our lives to a later day or date, which usually never happens.

Now more than ever, it is important that we learn how to remain attached yet detached and to detach yet being attached.

You would certainly be wondering why on one hand I am talking about family, togetherness, love, care etc. and on the other hand I am talking about "attach yet remain detached and detach yet remain attached".

Why is that so? I will tell you:

We are humans and not robots. We have feelings and that is what differentiates us from machines. Hormones like dopamine, which is closely related to an individual's personality and oxytocin, which drives the longing for re-bonding with the same person, cause us to attach ourselves to people and feelings, most especially, a partner, amongst other hormones.

This is why we attach ourselves and happiness with people, positions, wealth and all kinds of materialistic things, desired or expected outcomes from life. When all or some of the things mentioned above are not achievable, this is when we feel bad and sad. This sadness can affect our wellbeing, stop us from functioning properly and even deteriorate our health and mental state. Detachment from people, positions, wealth and materialistic desires or expected outcomes is vital to stay focused and keep our identity intact. At the same time, attachment is necessary for a beautiful life.

I am trying to explain that you should live your life, make friends, attach to relatives, with your family, your in-laws and friends. We are human, and we have to attach remembering there is a possible end in mind.

So how do we attach yet remain detached?

It is simple, take in the fact that life happens; children will leave home someday, friends will travel, you will get a new job or a business and move to a new area, parents will have to leave us someday, our life partner will leave us alone one day on this earth and this should not make us sad or depressed. Rather, we should live each moment to the fullest with our dear ones and not think much about the future because we know that whatever has come to exist on this earth shall certainly come to an end one day. Then why think of the end or worry about it.

For example, when a young lady gets married, she will leave her parents' house for the groom's house and become part of his family. This happens in India, and I believe it happens in other parts of the world too.

We all know that the daughter and father relation is one of the sweetest relationships in the world. You also know that your daughter will one day have to leave your house and go to her husband's house to start a new life there. So you attach with her yet remain detached because you know that she has to leave for her husband's house one day. You should shower your love and care towards her without letting her know that you are aware that she has to go far from you one day and you are already mentally prepared for it.

For instance, when my son was eighteen, I knew he had dreams of going to the United States to study. So when he cleared his A-level exams, I knew he would have to follow his dreams and leave us behind. This knowledge made me prepare myself for that day. I changed my approach; I attached myself to him and yet remained detached. He is my son, my only son. I love him but I want the best for him so I cannot hold him back and as such, I cannot suffer emotionally to stop him from his happiness.

You should be ready for such outcomes and embrace them when they do come so it does not affect your personal life; it should not negatively impact you. I have seen a lot of people, my self-included, that really changed after losing a loved one. I was very close to my mother and I think I got really disturbed for a very long period of time after losing my mother. So when you get into that kind of situation, it is important that you do not lose your core identity, you should not lose yourself; your health, your motto, your goal, your mission and most especially, you should not lose your mind.

You should show your love, compassion and emotions towards all your relations and let these relations feel that you really care for them and you are really attached to them. Yet you should have a possible end in mind because whatever has come to an existence has to go off one day, so, yet remain detached.

Now let me talk about your being detached yet remaining attached.

We normally attach ourselves to our materialistic goals like a good car, to a house, to good living, a good job, money, or/ and to a salary, but it is important that the attachment to these materialistic things, when not available, should not affect your emotional, physical and mental health. This is because you should know that positions, money, luxuries, stardom of life, everything has a shelf life and one day, either they will not be with you, or you will not be with them, and this should not impact you adversely. So, live life everyday rather than preserving it for the future.

You should not show your love, passion and attachment ONLY towards your materialistic desires because it will impact your personal life. All those materialistic achievements are just an outcome of your goals, set by you and you were able to achieve it because of your disciplined daily routine towards achieving them. However, running after them at the cost of you, your health, happiness and relatives is not advisable at all.

Though having materialistic goals are very important in life, one should remain detached from them and just focus on daily routines which will eventually take you towards them. One day either those things will not remain with you or they will remain with you but you will not be in a position to enjoy them because of your health, age, and interest. So you should remain detached from those materialistic desires yet remain attached. It will help you balance your professional and personal life.

There is a very thin line between attach and detach, and it can be quite tricky to define. It is a combination of science, art and commerce, wherein one should know the formula of striking a balance between both of them, an art of not letting others know about this trick and finally be aware of the break-even point between the two of them.

Life is generally about holding on to something, but you will find harmony when you can let go. Many spiritual teachings tell us about detachment because attachments can be so strong they make us lose control of ourselves. We give our control to that attachment and, as such, give away our happiness. These kinds of attachments take control of our lives; it takes our will power.

Note that being detached does not mean you should not have a sweet, healthy, and passionate relationship with people. It does not mean you should not buy your dream car or go for your dream house. It just means you should learn to let go when you have to and take it in good spirit.

We must learn the art of attaching yet remaining detached and detaching yet remaining attached. This state helps eliminate negative feelings like jealousy, envy, fear, anxiety, and hopelessness from our lives. Understand the outcomes of your attachment, and you will understand how to balance the two – attach and detach.

So ask yourself, what are you presently attached to, and how are you going to detach from it without compromising the attachment? Then what are you currently detached from, and how are you going to remain attached to it without compromising on the outcome.

"Trying to bring perfection into the various roles we play, leads us towards imperfections in life" - Rajeev Dua

Chapter 4

Life is like a movie, enjoy it!

Think about your favourite movie star and now think of his/her top three movies, were the roles in all three movies similar, or were they different?

Most often than not, a movie star has to act in various movies simultaneously so as to meet up with the deadline. However, I wonder if any of the roles affects the other as they play them simultaneously.

The secret of becoming a successful film star is to be as natural as possible and leave the character you played behind the very moment you are out from the movie set. Otherwise, one role will have an impact on another, which will affect the natural character of the film star; as a result it will impact his/her performance.

Do you think our lives are somewhat similar to this?

Our lives are like a movie and we play so many roles simultaneously. Some of the roles are born out of a routine while others, out of what is expected of us; but how much of it is truly who we are?

It is just like the movie, Multiplicity where the lead actor was cloned into many variations of himself. These clones helped him play so many different roles in his life (on screen), but each personality was different from the other based on the role they played.

In real life, a man plays the role of a father, brother, a husband, a son, a son-in-law, a brother-in-law, father-in-law, an uncle, a friend, a boss, a subordinate, a mentor, a mentee, a student, a colleague, a businessman and a customer, etc. Each role he plays calls for the character and emotions elicited. The roles are never completely alike and each person that is on the receiving side sees the individual from a unique perspective, yet this person plays all the roles simultaneously.

Just think for a moment, do you not play almost all the above roles simultaneously? Do you not try to be perfect in each role to satisfy the person you are playing the role for? So, this perfection brings out the imperfections in this journey called life.

For example - It is difficult (but not impossible) for a lady to play the role of a good daughter and also remain a good sister-in-law to her brother's wife and also remain a good sister to her brother. It is also challenging for a lady to become a wife, be a good daughter in-law and remain a good mother.

Some of our relationships will certainly not be as happy or as successful as others, in spite of our efforts though given in utmost sincerity; therefore it should not have adverse impact on the remaining relations because it is quite natural for such to happen.

We all look towards perfection in making everyone happy and as a result, we measure our impact on all our relationships and label or tag ourselves as either successful or unsuccessful. This ultimately impacts on our confidence. In it all, we lose our own identity, we forget our own strengths and start focusing on our weaknesses instead.

We should look at our inputs without worrying about the output. Most of the time, we concentrate more on the output rather than focusing on input and as a result, we are not able to perform well in any of the roles we play.

One should try and perform all the roles with utmost sincerity, honesty, love and passion, without worrying about the output (result). It is quite natural that you would not be able to satisfy all your roles because you are not a perfectionist. Stop taking yourself so seriously.

In this movie called life, we play so many roles and because of the involvement in so many roles, we lose our own identity. Trying to fit into these roles takes us away from who we truly are because we are not paying attention to who 'we are', but paying attention to who we ought to be, based on whoever is on the receiving end. That is why some people perceive you to be good while some perceive you to be bad. While one calls you a saint, somewhere else, another calls you a demon.

To some you are friendly, to others you are a snob. To your wife you are a darling and to your subordinates you are an evil boss. Different roles yet the same person; who are you?

As I have mentioned earlier, life is like a movie, focus on your deeds or input and your output will automatically be taken care of. Enjoy your life like a movie and do not take too much to heart.

You have been covered by layers, layers from society, from your home, your upbringing, your religion, your friends, your peers, your sibling, your wife, your husband, your children, your teachers, your colleagues, your handyman, etc. These layers have clouded you such that you cannot define the person that you are now.

If I should ask you to peel off these layers one by one as if peeling off skin from an onion, what will be the core found sitting, lonely in the middle? That person will be the true you.

Do not stop the reel, keep acting, life is as simple as you can make it to be. I have come to realize that in playing any of the roles assigned to me, I have to give my best performance. I do not need to cram the lines as it can be improvised. Flexibility is needed to enjoy life.

I have also learnt that the script can be flipped to suit my personality so when I am struggling with a line I can just go back to who I am and try to find out what role best suits this new character. It is not hard as we think; life is not hard as we think.

We just have to learn how to play each part. Learn to act with each supporting actor and how to carry the lines onto the next scene and the next, till the movie ends.

There is no 're-take' in life but you can have many 're-takes' in a movie. So, prepare yourself well for the movie called life. Give it your best shot without trying to be a perfectionist. Focus on your input and, last but not the least, enjoy it!

In the process of only satisfying others, you will lose your own identity. Live for everyone but love yourself.

You are creating a blockbuster movie called "Life" and YOU are the SUPERSTAR in it. – Rajeev Dua

"What brought you here, cannot guarantee you getting where you want to be" - Rajeev Dua

Chapter 5

Learn from Nature

Most times, you find people trying to recall who their first teacher was, however, most of us tend to forget that if there is someone who taught us our first lesson, it is the nature.

What does it mean to learn from the nature? It basically means to understand nature's behavior. Today when I was taking a walk, I saw a lot of mango leaves lying on the ground below a mango tree whereas, a month before I saw a lot of unripe mangos on this particular tree.

So taking a cue from nature; once a tree bears fruit and is loaded with them, nature will make sure it sheds all the weak leaves. The weak leaves will drop after the fruits have been plucked or after they fall off. After the weak leaves have dropped, fresh leaves will emerge and when they mature, we will see flowers emerge. These flowers will eventually produce new fruits and the cycle will repeat all over again. This cycle of nature repeats itself consistently, year in year out, without compromising the output.

 Do we really live like this? No, we do not.

As we grow, we develop certain habits and these habits eventually form a certain lifestyle for ourselves. These habits mostly don't change because we are averse to any kind of change. We keep on repeating these habits for our entire lives and after a certain age and time, we begin to have regrets; we have a sense of un-fulfillment, hence losing our happiness.

You have been doing the same thing, following the same routine, living with the same personality throughout your life; you have got into a comfort zone which does not allow you to change. Learn from nature - a tree will yield fruits and afterwards shed its old and weak leaves, because they have served their purpose for that cycle and hence will not be useful for the new phase the tree is about to begin. The old and weak leaves must be shed in order for new leaves to grow. Everything has a time and a season. If a tree does not shed the old leaves, it will not get fruits in the next season.

Similarly, in you there are so many skills, qualification, habits and knowledge, some of which are relevant and others irrelevant requiring change because life is not static. It is continuously moving and changing. Things which are relevant to you today might not be relevant to you tomorrow and vice versa.

The way a tree sheds its old leaves so that new leaves can come on board in other to bear fruits afresh, is the same way you will not be able to bear good fruits or achieve your full potential unless you shed your old ways and do away with those unnecessary weights that no longer serve you any purpose. Do away with unnecessary burdens, routines, skills, knowledge which are not relevant today. You have to let them go to create space for new leaves which can be by developing new skills, acquiring new techniques, new knowledge, and new habits or replacing old routines with new ones. If you do not do so, you will lose your sense of purpose, and you will not be able to grow because obsolete techniques, knowledge, and attitude will not take you to the desired destination; you will repent later with regrets and no sense of fulfillment. Always remember, learn from nature for she is the best teacher.

When I moved to Lagos (Nigeria) from India, it was a different world altogether. Different people, different cultures, technology, environments, languages, different ways of working, different market dynamics, etc. I quickly understood the need of the hour and promptly shredded off my knowledge and experience of India and learnt several new personal and business skills that were essential to succeed. If I had continued with my style of working in India based on my experience, I would not have had these successful two years in Lagos as a part of my Legacy.

Nature is indeed the best teacher; if you look at a massive tree in all its magnificence, you might be tempted to forget that the glorious beauty before you was once a tiny seed or plant. From a seedling or sapling, it becomes a plant, from plant to a tree, then it starts bearing flowers and then fruits at maturity. The best thing about nature that I intend to relate with humans is that the more the tree grows taller, bigger, and stronger till it starts bearing fruits, the more it gets connected to its roots and the soil.

If a tree becomes huge and starts bearing large quantities of fruits but is not connected to the soil, its foundation, or its roots, what will happen to that tree? We know that inevitably it will wither and die. Nature has made it so. Irrespective of a tree's height, its propensity to grow, and biological makeup, if it is not connected to the soil or its roots (which is its foundation), it will die. Naturally, the more a tree grows to maturity, the more it spreads its roots into the soil; these are the essentials for a tree's healthy growth.

Now let us relate this to humans. As we transition from childhood to adulthood, we lose the connection to our foundation; we delude ourselves into believing we know everything, we become arrogant and lack empathy towards people. We carry a massive load of our ego with us; we think things occur based on luck, good or bad, we take things for granted, and in that way, we lose connections to our roots. Irrespective of your level of growth, stage, position, and status in life, it is imperative that you remember that you will not be here forever. One day you will exit this stage that is your life, which is why you must be humble, deep-rooted, and remain down to earth.

You need to stay connected to your roots. Remember who you were as a child, the things that excited you and made you happy; these are your foundations, your roots. Remember your family, childhood friends, and/or colleagues, remember your teachers, mentors, and coaches who helped you become what you are today. If you are connected to your roots, you will not get lost in life, you will always stay grounded and rooted to your foundation. You will be able to fulfill all your responsibilities with happiness and pleasure, you will not see your responsibilities as a burden or pressure and the best part is you will know who you truly are.

Look at the beauty of nature, every element of nature has got certain unique characteristics to it. That element of nature would not have that essence of uniqueness if it loses its core characteristics. For example, salt with its unique characteristic of a salty taste, irrespective of its location, be it in the sea, food or a cosmetic product; it retains its taste, the sourness.

Take a mango too for example. It is sweet and a little tangy but it is mostly known for its sweetness. Now imagine you are eating a tasteless mango. You will not have more than a bite because a tasteless mango is strange to you. Take a look at water, which is colorless and quenches your thirst. Now imagine drinking colored water or water that does not quench your thirst; how would you feel?

Imagine if all these elements of nature do not retain their core characteristics, would you have the same respect, affection or love for it? So, every component of the universe has a set of unique features that defines it; and all over the world, it maintains these characteristics.

A human being also has specific universal characteristics, which most often than not, are entirely forgotten in the journey of life, as our actions are dictated by the way society wants us to behave. For instance, you might play a certain sport, not because you like it, but because when you socialize, the people you associate with play that sport. Inevitably, you behave and live your life based on what people want or expect of you – some call this peer pressure. Same goes to situations; we behave the way situations dictate for us. Circumstances dictate and make us act in a particular way so that we attain a certain position, and in the process of doing all this, we completely forget our core characteristics. Therefore, our existence also gets reduced, and later we blame it on life and luck.

Nature and its elements keep their core characteristic alive irrespective of age, weather, environment, atmosphere, and situations. Nature does not lose its core characteristics, no matter what; therefore, as humans, we should also know our core strengths, our likes, our dislikes, and the reason for our happiness, amongst other things, and we should not lose them. We should not forget them on account of difficult situations. Yes, we can adapt or acquire a new skill or characteristics based on the situation without compromising our core characteristics.

When you lose your core characteristics, you actually lose the essence of your life and you get lost in the journey of life. If you keep your core characteristics intact, the way nature does, irrespective of the situation and environment, believe me, you will live a life with joy and happiness.

"You cannot always choose the people around you, but you can definitely choose to be or not be influenced by them" - Rajeev Dua

Chapter 6

Your surroundings really matter

When you were born, you were raw and formless, like clay. That clay is later molded into a vessel and the task of forming that clay into a vessel is not the accomplishment of one person. There were several people contributing to making that clay into a vessel. For example, when you were born, you were surrounded by your parents and relatives, as you grew you became surrounded by friends, teachers, colleagues, acquaintances along with your family and relatives.

I remember my childhood days in school. I was really fond of playing volleyball and cricket but my school did not have a cricket team, they just had a volleyball team, and since I was surrounded by only people who played volleyball I gradually lost interest in cricket and was focused more towards volleyball. So grew my love for volleyball till I got to high school where I finally became a significant player for my team. My surroundings in school determined my interest and caused my love for volleyball to blossom. This interest in volleyball has spun through time, from my childhood into adulthood. From the lack of a cricket team in my school to being in the midst of only volleyball players, all these combined to form and increase my love for volleyball. So, in essence, what I am saying is that your surroundings really matter in shaping you into who you become as a person. They determine a lot in forming your personality and interests as an individual. Yes, it also goes without saying that your interest and capabilities determines your rate of success along with your surroundings.

As I grew further, from my eighth to twelfth standard, which are the formative years in a child's life, I realized that I was among the five best students in my class, and the five of us were inclined towards commerce and business studies, so we all became friends. It was only natural that a strong bond of friendship was formed amongst us. We used to study and hang out together, and then I realized that because our tastes were similar, study patterns similar and we were fond of hanging out together, we had therefore influenced each other in behavior and interests.

Today as I write, out of my five friends, four are chartered Accountants while I majored in business administration after graduating from the commerce stream. Basically, all of us have finance or business backgrounds and we are all successful. So, your surroundings and the company you keep really matter in shaping you into who you become as an individual.

Today, when you look at yourself, your personality and the person you have become in life, you will observe that there are a lot of people who had in one way or the other affected your life by making an impact, positively or negatively. You also learnt a lot of good or bad things during your teenage years and they were taught to you by some of your friends, seniors or acquaintances.

You will also recall that when you were young, your parents used to say that the friends or company you keep really mattered and you now find yourself saying the same to your kids as parents now. This is because you know that people can influence you and vice versa if you spend enough time with them. What you will become is not only dependent on what you study but will also be influenced by the company that surrounds you and friends you study and hang out with.

So, as you are aware that you cannot choose the people or surroundings around, still you can choose who can or cannot impact your personality by spending time and giving attention to your chosen ones.

As adults when we recall our childhood days, we usually say that nothing can beat our childhood days, because we remember our childhood friends and say no one compares to them. We recall how precious that friendship was to us, we go down memory lane and recall the cherished moments we had as kids with our friends. The reason for this is because at that point in time, we were carefree and we liked our friends, not because of what they had or did not have, we did not draw conclusions towards their efforts or any of their activities, we just liked them the way they were. That is why as children our friendship circle was actually selfless with zero selfishness and zero strings attached to it.

Therefore it is important when you grow to always remember and care about your childhood friends because they know "YOU" as a person; because they know your strengths and weaknesses as an individual and they are there to always remind you who you truly are.

The reason you tend to lose yourself and your identity, is because as you journey through life and expand your relationships by making new friends, professional friends or social friends, getting into romantic relationships, getting married, and so on, your circle increases (It is quite natural). This is why it is important that you remember by recalling those childhood friends who had been with you from your early beginning; put in extra effort to be in touch with them. Do not lose contact with them because they are the ones who will always remind you of who you truly are; they are part of your root and foundation. By so doing, in your journey through life you will not get lost, you will grow and achieve all your materialistic goals and still, you will not lose yourself.

When I moved to Lagos, my intention was to move with my family but for some reasons I could not move my family, so I ended up staying alone in a new city. This was the time wherein my childhood friends, Kamal, Ravi, Suresh and Raghav sitting back home in India took care of me in Lagos. They motivated me whenever the chips were down due to my loneliness, they could sense even the smallest change in my voice and would motivate me to stay focused on the aim of coming to Lagos, Nigeria.

So it is important for you to retain your two close childhood friends, those who actually know "you" and they will not allow you to lose your core identity in the journey called life.

In the last few years because of my routine and job transfers, I could not develop the habit of writing and reading. Though I had always wanted to write a book, this book you are now reading was actually conceived in my mind about five years ago, but I was not able to write it in all that time. It was not until I came to Lagos, Nigeria that I was really triggered to start writing and this was caused by the fact that I was surrounded by people that had the same interests and passion for writing. I met Dr Batth and also met my storyteller Sush (Suziette) and several other people who were in the profession of book writing.

So, when I made friends with them, I got to know their profession/work and we started indulging in discussions related to the thoughts of my book and during those intellectual discussions; my old dream of writing a book got triggered. The dream to write that I had always kept at the back of my mind came back and my being surrounded by these good people spurred me into action, motivated me to pen down my thoughts and hence the birth of this book.

When I met them I quickly moved towards my interest which had been lost in the journey of life; I quickly grabbed the opportunity and started writing this book. I am forty five now but the idea to write this book was conceived when I was forty but I could not write it then. Yet at the age of forty five I have been able to write this book because of my surroundings and the people in it. These people became the catalyst I needed to push me to write. They motivated me to get into a position where I mentally prepared myself and took time out of my so-called busy schedule so that I can invest myself in this book.

It is important for you to surround yourself with people, not because of their financial strengths or because of their social status but because they have the same values and interest you possess and your souls connect with each other.

I have always believed that we cannot really choose people around us, we will meet people with a lot of similarities and dissimilarities. Eventually people with the same interests, hobbies, personalities and values tend to come close to each other and become friends. These set of people are the ones who will have a great influence in making who "you" are today.

Let us look at nature and observe the way a lotus blossoms. A lotus grows in dirty water. It is surrounded by extremely dirty water but connected to the soil beneath the dirty water which does not allow the lotus to get detached but keeps it connected and in place with the dirty water. This connection eventually helps the lotus blossom. Similarly, your surroundings or friends will always guide you to stay on the right track and will not allow you to lose your core identity, irrespective of all kinds of odds. They will ensure that you achieve all your goals and you do not lose your "own self" in the journey called life.

This tells us that your associations, friendships and surroundings really matter, so distinguish between your friends and acquaintances, ensure that you are connected with those friends who bring out the best in you and impact you positively. That way you will not get negatively influenced by people who should remain mere acquaintances. So, it is necessary for you to understand the difference between friends and acquaintances, it does not mean that acquaintances are not really important in life, they are, but one should know the difference between them. It is going to help you live your life in a better way.

When I first came to Lagos, Nigeria, I fell in love with the country. This Country is simply beautiful. I love its people. Everything in this Country is so easily available; here you find the cheapest liquors, cigarettes, company, clubs and many more. I met people with such interests and priorities, I could have easily chosen to be surrounded with them and start achieving my materialistic goals; be happy with those so-called socially acclaimed people and spend my time, money and energy on the cheap things which are easily available.

Let me be honest, like every normal human, I also got distracted for a while but later, my surroundings helped pull me back from the distraction and moved me towards that right path. I also met people who were intellectually strong, had similar interests of writing, having fun within set boundaries, nature loving people, sharing the same values as mine.

I always remained focused on my aim of coming to Nigeria and I was excited, I really wanted to give back something good and positive to society in the form of a book that captures the feelings I have; my experiences, my knowledge and the life that I have lived, so that the society can benefit from it. As a result I chose to be surrounded with people like Dr. Batth, Ms. Sush (Suziette), Mr. Prashant, and Mr. Mathew - the book is the result of my surroundings. Thanks to each one of them.

So, it is important for you to look at your surroundings irrespective of age. If you look at my father, he is seventy-five years old and at his age, he has never used any kind of smartphone. Yet when my son went to the United States of America, my father wanted to do a WhatsApp video call with my son, but he was unable to do so on a regular mobile phone, so he bought a smartphone to enable him speak to his grandson, and he learnt that at such an old age. This was made possible because of his morning walk-friends, who taught and motivated him to buy and use a smartphone. So, the surroundings really matter irrespective of your age.

The beauty of life is to find like-minded people amongst the huge crowd and achieve your spiritual, financial and social goals which make you happy and keep your core identity intact.

**"Stardom is just a chapter of your life,
not the entire book" - Rajeev Dua**

Chapter 7

The Stardom

Every individual reaches a peak in his or her life, though the meaning of the peak and its intensity varies for each person. The peak of our professional life is called "Stardom."

Let me explain a little more about it.

Stardom is when we reach the peak of our careers or whatever we do, or the phase where we exceed our financial or social goals; having an identity that our family and friends are really proud of. Stardom is when we reach the topmost phase of fame.

Every individual passes through the stardom phase of their lives, though the meaning and tenure of stardom might vary for each individual. The start of the stardom also actually varies for individuals. For example, you might reach the peak of your professional career at age thirty or forty, and it can also start at the age of twenty-five and last till you are in your forties or fifties or even later - it all depends on the individual.

Stardom is a phase that everybody desires to experience in life. Take me for instance, I started my career at the age of twenty, and from then, I have never looked back. I have been promoted every alternate year in every company I have worked in. I achieved my personal goals, my professional goals, and claimed an excellent status in society. Many people aspire to do an expatriate assignment or import/export business to earn a lot of money and fame. By the grace of God, I am presently doing a foreign assignment in Lagos, Nigeria. For me, by the grace of God, my stardom phase is still ongoing.

What really happens during the stardom phase? During the stardom phase, you grow consistently until you reach the top of your career. Stardom teaches you many good things, it gives you a sense of achievement, satisfaction, and fulfillment; it also teaches you a lot of bad things that are not right.

Stardom teaches you to remain above the average people, learn new things, unlearn things that are not required, remain competitive and give your best in whatever you do. It also forces you to compromise with your health; you compromise with your relationships, become more materialistic, judgmental, and sympathetic instead of being empathetic. Finally, you forget to manage defeats and forget that not every battle is supposed to be fought and won; sometimes not participating in a battle is also a winning strategy.

When you are engrossed so much in your stardom phase, you get so busy with your work. You have your targets which are constantly changing with every achievement, and you also know that every second, there is a new challenge to fulfill, thus you welcome those challenges; in doing so, you tend to compromise with your health.

Money and work become more important than health, you start ignoring your basic exercise regime at the cost of your so-called stardom. You also tend to compromise with your family and friends and eventually you will compromise with yourself.

You forget being empathic, forget your own journey, the

journey you took to scale up. This makes you see everyone as your competition rather than finding a way to help them grow too. Though few of us will still be sympathetic towards people, especially those who are not at par with us, yet most of us completely lose our empathy. We completely forget our struggling phase, we forget the struggle that we have undergone to reach the stardom phase and become judgmental about people and label them as either successful or unsuccessful without having any authority to do it.

We get so engrossed in that rat race of stardom that we tend to forget everything around us. We get into an artificial glittery world that usually does not last forever; still, we want to become a part of it, at the cost of our own foundation and eventually fall once the stardom is no longer with us.

We have to remember that nothing is permanent in life, including STARDOM. We should always stay connected to our roots or foundation (Knowing our true friends who are not associated to us because of our stardom, knowing things which makes us happy and knowing our own strengths) so that when we are not at the peak of our lives, when we are no more famous and desired as we were earlier, we will still stand on our own feet and not fall.

Believe me, most of us go through this phase in our lives and fall because we are not connected to our own roots.

There is an ecosystem or life cycle for everything. There will be a time when we are part of the ecosystem; that is the phase when we are loved, famous, desired, admired and accepted by the society. Then a time will come when we move out of the ecosystem. Most of us fail to stand on our own feet when we are out of the ecosystem because our STARDOM foundation was weak. This is because we did not stay connected to our own roots during our STARDOM period.

We must remember that everything has got a shelf life. All of us have one. Every living thing and non-living thing has got a shelf life; even I have got a shelf life too, so does stardom. If I have a shelf life, my stardom cannot have a shelf life longer than me, people will remember me for my legacy, but my stardom will die the day I exit this world.

It is paramount to understand that stardom will not be there forever, so endeavor to maximize all opportunities available in the stardom phase. You should capitalize on that stardom phase, but always remember to strike a balance between the things you are willing to compromise on during your stardom phase and what you cannot compromise.

This is important because if you compromise with the essential things of life, it will be too late to correct your mistakes once your stardom fades off. For instance, if you compromise on valuable things like family, friends, your health and your hobbies, when the stardom is no longer there it might be too late for you to again get back to them in life.

Imagine if your stardom fades at fifty-five, it will be hard but not impossible for you to regain good health at this time. You will be sad and start thinking and regretting the loss of your hobbies, health, family and friends.

Yes, we will and should all have stardom in our life; this is why we are here, but it is important to strike a balance between stardom and the things / people that are valuable to us, so that stardom does not dominate the softer aspect of our lives. We must know how to strike a balance between stardom and our normal life.

It is mostly during the stardom period many of us become arrogant. The over confidence sometimes is perceived as arrogance in our behavior. We have to be extremely careful during the stardom phase and not lose our humanity because stardom forces us towards being proud and arrogant about our achievements. We should also remember our struggling time and remember those people who helped us during the days of our struggle so that when we reach our stardom, we can also become a role model for others.

We should understand that stardom is nothing more than the output of our input. Our input is basically our own effort, hard work, passion, willingness to grow and being FUTURE READY. When we achieve stardom, people start liking us, people start liking our work, we are admired, our work is acknowledged, our families like us, we are socially accepted, we acquire more competencies, and our materialistic goals are well achieved.

Therefore, focus should always be on your input. Whether the outcome is stardom or not does not really matter, you should always focus on the input that really gives you happiness. If your input is in the right direction, you will definitely get great output and your stardom will be long-lasting and happy. You will not only enjoy long-lasting stardom, but also strike a balance between your stardom, yourself and your family / friends.

You should also remember to accept defeat, as all battles cannot and should not be won. However, you should learn from your defeats, to make you a better professional. If you are connected to your own roots then it does not really matter whether you are or are not a part of the STARDOM ecosystem. You should focus more on your input; stardom is just an output, so do not really worry about your outcome.

"A balance between you and your surroundings
is the key to a happy life" - Rajeev Dua

Chapter 8

Selfies of life

A focus on one's self is called a selfie. Is it not?

A selfie is a terminology used to take a digital self-portrait photograph, typically taken with a digital camera or smartphone, which may be held in the hand or supported by a selfie stick.

So take a selfie; pout, pose and snap.

When taking a selfie, you usually concentrate the camera on yourself and also on the surroundings near you. No one takes a selfie in an uncomfortable place. So yes, without thinking, you concentrate on your surroundings before taking a picture to ensure it will beautify you and create an appealing aesthetic.

Usually we change to many angles and poses in different styles till the time we feel that we and our surroundings are in sync with each other and we take several selfies till we get the perfect shot. Sometimes life becomes so monotonous that we feel like looking at ourselves from a different angle to ensure that we and our surroundings look beautiful.

Our lives should also be lived in such a manner - from the moment we look beautiful to ourselves, till the time we are satisfied with our surroundings. We should keep on trying hard to keep ourselves and surroundings in sync, in order to have that perfect selfie.

While taking a selfie, your focus is largely on you and your surroundings. So, life should also be lived a similar way. Unfortunately, most of the time your focus is more on the surroundings around you rather than on yourself. As a result, you make everyone happy without even knowing that you are not happy with yourself; but this realization comes to you at a later stage of your life.

It is imperative to focus on your own likes, dislikes, priorities, and preferences so as to make your life beautiful. You will not take a selfie unless you look beautiful in the selfie.

So, always take care of yourself while being concerned about others too.

A selfie is introspection; you are not only evaluating yourself but you are also looking at the people around you, the places, the things you have done and changes you have made through life. The circumstances you find yourself in and those around you, you will want them to look beautiful and you would want to look good in them; there is no harm in that.

When you do introspection on yourself, you tend to keep track on you, your core strengths and values. You become focused and have a direction which is not easily swayed by others.

However, while taking care of yourself, you are to take care of everyone too; your parents, your spouse, your colleagues, your children, etc. Yes, you are to take care of them too while taking care of you but do not lose focus. Do not forget to be in a place of self-awareness.

Your surroundings should not be happy at the cost of your own happiness. You should not lose yourself while making people happy. This is why you should always take a selfie of life.

"A selfie is nothing but self-care and self-care isn't being selfish." – Rajeev Dua

Mind you self-care is not selfish. Selfish is when you take care of yourself by harming the people around you emotionally or physically, but in self-care, you take care of yourself and you care for every one too, and this is what makes life beautiful.

There is nothing wrong in self-care. For example when you are on an airplane, the flight attendant teaches you that in an emergency situation, you should put on your mask first before you help put it on your children or the next vulnerable person.

The same caution is given when you go for a boat cruise. The boat cruise captain or coach will tell you to put on your life jacket first before you help someone else put on theirs, even if they are your children. This does not mean you do not care for them, nor does it mean the flight attendant or boat cruise instructor wants you to be selfish. No, it is just telling you that you have to care for yourself first to be able to care for others.

If you are able to care for yourself, you will be able to care for your surroundings - your family, your children, your friends, your colleagues and everyone and everything around you.

This is saying you can take care of others by being your best self. Take care of yourself so that you are healthy, alert, and focused to be at your best. One cannot take care of others when they are down or unhealthy emotionally, physically or mentally.

So take a selfie often, look at yourself and evaluate. Are you and your surroundings complimenting each other? Are you where you want to be? Do you like what you have become? Do you like the job you are doing and are you on the right career path?

These questions are essential in life.

In building a harmonious life, you have to be happy with who you are and who you are becoming. This will help you be focused, productive and emotionally, physically and mentally strong enough to support others.

Have you paid attention lately to your surroundings and are you happy with what you see? Do a mental throw back on who you thought you would be, and compare it to who you are now.

Life's selfie is important to daily living. Do not take it for granted, sit up, strike a pose, take a selfie and evaluate. Look at your surroundings while at it, be sure you are looking beautiful and taking a beautiful picture.

Always be cautious of the fact that YOU should also look good in the selfie and compliment the surroundings.

**"Dreams can only be fulfilled and enjoyed
while you are awake" - Rajeev Dua**

Chapter 9

I wish I could have

If I ask you today to relive the past life as it concerns some relationships and moments, I bet you would like to relive or rewrite some.

You also know that there is an end to everything and there is a shelf life for everything you see around you. Everything you see has to perish one day; everything has an end. When you know that there is an end to everything then why do you still take relatives, moments, achievements, success, failures, and your friends, even yourselves for granted? Why do you not remain happy and calm in all situations and with people around you?

In the fast paced journey called life we become so busy in our regular stuff that we tend to forget our own efforts.

At a young age, some of us did not go out to play, instead we kept ourselves occupied inside with video games. In our teens we focused on marks instead of our studies. Even in our twenties, we focused more on getting paid than on learning the job. In our thirties we became so career conscious that we tended to forget our families (parents, wife, kids, etc.) then in our forties we forget our own selves and become victims of this materialistic world. Then later in our fifties , we start to recall our past years and start saying "Oh I wish!"

How did we end up this way? When we all know that one day we all shall become old and then the inevitable will happen. There is only one eternal truth for living things and that is death; the end of life. With this knowledge, why do we then wait to become old and weary before we repent?

In the fast paced journey called life, due to your so-called busy schedule, you do not spend quality time with your own self, children, parents, and spouse. You do not cherish your small and big achievements. You do not pursue your hobbies, likes or do everything on your bucket list. You forget that all these relatives, achievements, hobbies and wish list shall die one day, and when they do, all you will have remaining with you will be your memories and you.

In life, I bet you all have had that moment when you wished for something you could have. I bet it happened often, like once a month, when you would say 'Oh, I wish I could travel' or 'Oh, I wish I could go back to my childhood' or 'Oh, I wish I would have taken that job', or 'Oh I wish I could spend time with my family', or 'Oh, I wish I could get one chance to live my teens', 'Oh I wish!'

We all wish we could go back in time to do something differently or in the case of losing a loved one, we wish we could have spent more time with them or given them so much more. We would even wish they could see us now, to make them proud.

I lost my mother seven years ago, and all I can do now is wish; I wish she could come back and see her children doing well, I wish I could spend time with her which I could not do in the fast-paced journey called life. I wish, I can eat meals cooked by her, she was the best cook in the world. I wish I could go on a small vacation with her to make her happy, go for a drive with her in a Jeep (She used to prefer Jeeps over normal cars). All these will remain a WISH, as she wouldn't be able to come back.

In this race called life, you tend to forget what is important. You are running and running and not looking or caring. One thing this present pandemic (COVID-19) has done, is that it has made the family unit closer again. It also made you aware of things you wanted to do and never had time to do.

Now that everyone is in doors, you can make that call that you wanted to make but never did due to work. Like today, I had the time to call and speak to my wife and son because I am working from home. I bet you too had time to check up on your family, especially on those far from you. Maybe this virus, though sad and has killed a lot of people, has a good side to it. It has brought us together once again. Showing us that what is really important is you and your "family".

The lockdown has enabled people to remain indoors playing board games like we use to do in the past, playing with family, and bonding like we should. We are taking time to get to know each other better, how we work, how we school, how we cook and how we relax. Most importantly, we have all understood that knowing yourself is the biggest asset that one can have.

You do not need a pandemic to remind you of what is important to you. You do not need an excuse to spend time with your family or check up on them. Just like you do not need to be far from them or lose them before you know what you want to do for them and with them, or to tell them you love them.

Do not let wishes have the better of you; do what you want to. I always say, live to make yourself happy, if you are happy, I am sure you will make others happy too. If you have a childhood hobby you miss, go back to it and I can assure you, it will make you happy; no one is stopping you but yourself.

I understand that we are humans and we all have certain commitments, some duties or responsibilities that we need to attend to, in order to make a living but my friend, you need to take time out to do things that gives YOU happiness. The one, two, three or four things you need to do for yourself before you are gone. Those things will make you happy and build your legacy, keeping you in the minds of people when you are gone. So just do them; do not let them die before you.

Legends and legacies are only formed when those legends pursue their passions which give them happiness. So, if you want to leave a legacy behind, you should do things that makes you happy. Legends are not born as legends, they become legends and create a strong legacy because they have outperformed others. Whatever they did, it gave them happiness.

Spend time with yourself, play those games, call those loved ones, and spend that quality time you need to spend with your parents, your wife, your children, your siblings, friends or whoever; spend that time. Even spend it with you, play that game, go for that job, bungee jump if you want; do all you need to, so you will not end up with the phrase - 'Oh I wish'.

We all know that the inevitable day will come someday, so why spend time wishing when you can spend the time doing? Go out, live life, enjoy yourself, live the best you can live and do all you would love to while here.

If you are young, think about your 30s, your 40s, your 50s, what would you like to do which gives you happiness and what would you like to achieve before you are that age; start preparing for them now. If you are mid-life, think about all you wish you had done and want to do before you are gone and do them NOW. There is no time but now.

I once read that at the end of your life, you will never regret not having passed one more test, not winning one more verdict, or not closing one more deal. You will regret time not spent with yourself, your husband/wife, a friend, a child, a parent and friends.

Turn your 'Oh I wish' to 'Yes I did' and see the best you emerge. Regrets are things we cannot take back, it weakens us and sometimes, changes us for good or for bad, mostly for bad. Emotions get killed because of regrets and we lose sight of what is important to us.

It is vital that in a busy schedule, you must find time for the people you love. You must find time for you and the things you love to do.

Do not wait for an external or internal epidemic to live your life; live your life now! There is no better time than now. Take care of yourself, go see that movie you always wanted to see, start that hobby you fancy, and propose to that girl you want to. Do not worry about the outcome; worry sets you back, and you achieve nothing. Nike, the apparel brand, understands this very well hence their slogan, 'Just Do It', because you will never know what you are capable of if you are only thinking about it and worrying about the outcome.

In the fast-paced journey called life, do not forget yourself while racing towards your materialistic goals. Celebrate your successes and failures, and along with it, spend time with your loved ones because one fine day, you will certainly not see them around. There is no way you can rewind your life to relive those moments. Live your life now, do not reserve it for the future.

Most significantly, do not take yourself for granted, do not take relationships for granted. Settle that fight now, visit your parents, kiss your child good night every night, talk to your spouse as much as you want to, go for that religious event or that social event, do all those activities that bring you happiness. Ensure you live your best life after this global lockdown. There is nothing worse than a mental lockdown, wherein you tell yourself you cannot, or there is still time, I will do it tomorrow. There is nothing called tomorrow, DO IT NOW.

"Copy to improvise not to paralyze"
- Rajeev Dua

Chapter 10

"What will people say?"

We encounter this question at least once every day and when we do, we pause a bit from whatever we are doing - sometimes that pause is logical for us and sometimes it is not.

As good human being it is important for us to have respect and regard towards people and ensure that our deeds do not, in any manner, hurt anyone's emotions or feelings. As long as you have such thoughts while taking your decisions that is fine. However, when you fail to make your decisions on the merit of the situation or circumstance but based on competition, jealousy, inferiority complex, or to prove yourself better, then your decision-making is faulty and will have a rather adverse impact on you. The facts are, most of us knowingly or unknowingly live our lives like this.

From time immemorial, people have taken critical life's decisions and made important choices based, not on their interests or desires, but on the question 'What will people say?'

Our family and our parents usually influence our decisions as kids and even when we become independent and go on to have our own children, we have always done things, made decisions and choices based on other people's influence. Most often we do not take decisions based on what is good for us, logical and is the need of the hour.

There are parents who choose their children's professions based on what other relative's children are pursuing or what their neighbours will say. Some parents even go to the extent of determining what a child should become because there is a close neighbour or relative or friend whose child is a seasoned lawyer, medical doctor or engineer. Such parents are willing to influence their children's professional choices on this basis, insisting their kids toe the same line as the kids of their relatives, neighbours and friends. Such parents will not allow their children to study what they want or have affinity for like accounting or marketing, because they are concerned about what people will say or what others are doing.

Parents usually take such decisions without being mindful of what the child is good at nor think of what might interest the child. There is no question of what will make the child happy, all that matters to these parents in making a decision for their kids, is what people will say.

Every individual has his or her own strengths, weaknesses and yet some go ahead and take decisions based on the dictates of society. They consider the needs and what looks good for the society and seek validation from people's commentaries. They fail to consider if such decisions are favourable to them in light of their strengths and weaknesses or if it is good for them in the long run, or even if the decisions are aligned with their interests.

We tend to get carried away by focusing mainly on what others are doing, how they are living their lives, what materialistic goals they are achieving, etc. It is from this we birth the syndrome of 'what will people say', when taking decisions or making choices that affects our lives. We find ourselves comparing our lives to others because we have shifted our focus from our OWN lives to the lives of others. When we lose that focus and start making decisions based on what people will say, we are no longer out to impress ourselves but to impress others and seek their validation for our existence. Everyone, be it a low, middle or a high class family, every member of society is somewhere taking decisions to impress others and not to make themselves happy.

There is no positive impact when we make decisions based on what people will say. There is no fulfilment when we make life choices based on what people will say. Later in the stage of life when the journey has led us to higher levels, we look back with regrets, we become remorseful wondering what we have done to our lives. We begin to regret those decisions we took based on what people will say, because we have discovered that it was neither our will nor our desire, it was not our lives, but by that time it will be too late.

It is imperative that you do not get swayed away by people's opinions or live your life based on them. Do not get carried away by the whims of society, do not let the lives of your acquaintances entice you to the point where you lose focus of your own life and start to live theirs. Do not get carried away by others, do what is good for you. You know what is good for you, you know what makes you happy, you know where and in what your own interests lie. Therefore take your decisions, make your choices based on your own desires and interests, not based on your friends', society's, relatives' or neighbours'. Now whether the decision is in respect to you, your children, your career, your family, your business, your wealth, your actions or your style of fashion, do what is good for you. Do not be bothered about what people will say, the decision is yours to make as it affects your life.

We can quote some examples of some successful business men, successful sports men and women, successful filmmakers, actors and TV stars. When you study their lives, you will observe that they became successful, not because they took decisions based on society's dictates, or what their neighbour did, nor did they consider the lives of their relatives. No, they took their decisions based on their own strengths. They focused on their strengths, they also knew their weaknesses, they knew exactly what to pursue in life because they were focused on themselves. They knew what they were good at because they were aware of their abilities through being focused on themselves. if they had not taken decisions or made life choices based on their strengths, weaknesses, likes and dislikes, then they would have not become the success stories that they are today.

A successful person becomes so when he or she creates his or her own path. When you follow a path created by someone else, you will confine yourself to only where that path leads, but on the contrary, when you concentrate on the path chosen by you, it will eventually lead you to your ultimate destination. So if you really want to be a successful person, choose your own path. Taking a path chosen by someone else is not entirely a bad thing to do, as long as it is based on your own interests, strengths and you are sure of reaching your ultimate destination. However, just taking someone else's path which is not aligned with your interests, will lead you to nothing but disaster; an unfulfilled life, loss of individuality and personality is the end result. Imitating or copying something is not entirely bad, sometimes it serves as a template, but one should be encouraged to create his or her own identity by being unique.

If you are not unique from others, you will not be able to fit in the ecosystem of this life. What I mean by ecosystem is that in life, there is a need, there is a consumer, there is a producer, there is a seller, there is a buyer etc. You need to understand this cycle and choose where to fit in. If your decision is not able to make you fit into the cycle (the ecosystem), the chances are you might not be able to reach your desired destination, whereas if you have understood the cycle well, then you will be able to fit into the ecosystem, be successful and happy.

If you just copy what others are doing, how they are living their lives, or you take certain actions based on what people will say, then you will neither truly be a successful nor a happy person in life. Create your own self-identity and stick to it, observe your strengths and weaknesses, choose your battles, take your decisions, make your choices so that you can create your own path. Do not confine yourself to limited paths that people have already taken, life itself is a self -discovery journey, find and discover your own path, the one best suited for you.

We make up the society we live in, this is a fact we are aware of, and so we cannot completely ignore the society, our family and our friends. However, in taking decisions and changing them based on what people will say in isolation, without looking at your own strengths is shooting yourself in your feet, such a decision will ultimately fail. I am not saying that we become like robots or start living in isolation and stop interacting with society, our friends, relatives and family. Yes, we live in the same society, we can observe what they are doing or not, but our decisions and choices should remain based on our strengths; our decisions should be based on our own way of thinking, they should not be coloured with what people will say. Ultimately my interests, my loans, everything is going to be paid by me, not by my friends, relatives or family, so if my responsibilities are solely mine, so should my decisions.

If a decision fails and it was a thoughtful one, that is fine. You should not get worried about taking a decision that could fail, there are lessons to be learnt from failing, and no success story is complete without mentioning the mistakes and failures therein. When we take the lessons learnt from failure, we get up better and stronger, we improvise and move on further. It is perfectly okay when you take a thoughtful decision based on your strengths, interests and still fail, but taking decisions based on what people will say or other people's likes and dislikes is not something I encourage or recommend.

So when you are able to concentrate on your own strengths, know what you are good at, and make your own decisions, you will be yourself, you will not lose yourself. You will not lose your identity and in the journey called life, you will be a successful and a happy person with your own identity

"Tomorrow will surely become today someday, today will surely become yesterday someday and yesterday will surely become history one day"
— Rajeev Dua

Chapter 11

My time will come one day

In life as you grow older, you grow with anticipation and hope that your time will come one day.

When you say 'your time', it means your good time, your favourable time, the time when your most precious and important dreams finally manifest, the time when all your desires materialize into reality.

When you were a child, you anticipated going to high school and college because you thought your good time would come then. Fast forward to college, you began to look forward to getting your Masters' degree, because you thought your good time would come then. Moving ahead, after you had gotten your Masters' degree, you predicted your good time would surely come when you start your first job or venture into a business. When you start your job/business and after completing your first few years, you would dream of having loads of money, and you will say to yourself again – 'My time will come when I have my first promotion and then I will have a good time'.

Then after spending another few more years at your job and you are now earning well, you will think about getting married. Then you will say that your time will come when you get a good spouse, you will have a good number of kids, and a beautiful family. At that time, when you are married and you have your kids, you once again say, "Let my kids grow up, they are young now so I have to really concentrate on their health and upbringing. A lot of time and energy is invested in raising kids, my good time will come when my kids are grown and become independent."

That time also comes and you say, "Let my kids study well and get some professional qualifications, my good time will start then, and I can finally relax and live my retired life peacefully and I will be dependent on my children to take care of me". So you go on and on in your life.

One day, a time comes when you complain regarding your ill health, maybe a pain in the left side of the chest, your family panics and calls a doctor who makes his diagnosis and informs you that your time has come and everyone is bewildered, wondering what the doctor means by 'Your time has come'. The doctor then says you are about to die and your time has come to leave this heavenly earth.

Throughout our lives we keep on thinking and waiting for our good time, and each time that comes, we keep on saying it is not the right time; we keep on postponing the celebration, we sit and wait for that so called good time. This is how most of us spend our entire lives and later have regrets for living our life in such a manner.

Definitions of a good time will vary from person to person. For some people, the achievement of their materialistic goal is a good time whereas for others, being in a happy state, pursuing their interests, having good family time, having good health, having respect in the society or being in a position to help others is a good time.

Once you know what good times mean to you then you have to

align your acts in line with your expectations. You have to change your working style, to bring fresh ideas, to live a disciplined life, you have to demonstrate a positive attitude towards your life. Then you will be able to achieve what you have desired, otherwise your entire life will pass by with you saying, "This is not the right time" or "My time will come one day". Eventually that time will come when you have to meet the creator of this universe and your soul will leave your body.

One has to earn that good time with proper hard work and dedication. Just sitting idle and thinking your good time will come will not make it so. You have to work hard and figure out the right path that leads to that good time for you; only then will you be able to reach and enjoy your good time.

Therefore, it is crucial that you remember that there is nothing like 'my good time will come'; you should enjoy and cherish each moment of your life, remain focused and self-content. Each day is a gift given by the almighty and you should thank him and utilize it to the fullest.

"There is nothing either good or bad, but our thinking made it so"- Shakespeare.

It is your state of mind that determines whether it is a good time or bad time. If you are contented, fulfilled and satisfied with your life, you will always consider yourself as having a good time and living the good life; but if you are dissatisfied, unfulfilled in your life and malcontent, you will always be unhappy, even your achievements will not bring you happiness in life.

As you grow older and move ahead in life you will keep on modifying and altering your materialistic goals and targets;

that is to say you keep on upgrading and that is fair. However, while you are upgrading your goals, your targets and your materialistic desires, you should also have a sense of satisfaction and contentment because whatever God has given you is more than you deserve. Always be thankful to God for whatever you have got - simply remain happy. If you have this kind of attitude, every time will be a good time for you; whereas when you lack this positive outlook on life, you will always be unhappy about what you have and this will leave you dissatisfied, discontent and in a state of always wondering when your time will come.

If you want to upgrade yourself you do it today. If you want to be rich you start today. If you want to start your yoga or spiritual session, you start today. If you want to keep yourself happy, it is today, there is nothing like, 'I will be happy tomorrow'. Nothing is tomorrow, nothing is worth more than today.

We live our entire lives, waste our entire years, days, months in thinking of tomorrow and stay without doing anything today; we only waste today by using it to think of tomorrow.

Spending your time thinking of tomorrow will not make your today; taking action today will make your today and eventually every day lived to the full will accumulate into weeks, months and years of your life. There is nothing called tomorrow, everything is today, if you want to acquire skills, you need to do it today. If you want to be happy, be happy today, if your state of mind says, 'Today I am not happy, tomorrow is going to be better', no, it has to be today.

Always focus on your deeds and remember your good time is directly proportional to your deeds. Whatever the situation is, be self-content for today. Yes, today is beautiful, tomorrow will be more beautiful. Have a positive attitude towards life, make use of your today and when you focus on today, your tomorrow will automatically be beautiful. There is nothing called tomorrow, everything is today and so, do it NOW!

Though there is no harm in having materialistic or non-materialistic desires but sacrificing and compromising your entire life in blindly chasing them is not an ideal way of living. Have your materialistic desires but remain happy and contented each day. Just focus on your daily routine and your strengths which will make you happy and lead you towards those desires, and even if you are not able to achieve them, you will never say that your time will come one day, because you have lived your life to the fullest while chasing your dreams.

When you are clear about your own goals and the path that will take you towards them, then I am pretty sure that you will not lose your identity while finding your definition of that good time. Most of us lose our core identity in finding the definition of our good time. Your journey of life will be more meaningful and content if you focus more on your inputs in life.

"Enjoy your today to make your tomorrow better; you cannot enjoy tomorrow without being contented today." – Rajeev Dua

"Adjust your personal and professional life in one cart because you can't drive two separate carts simultaneously" - Rajeev Dua

Chapter 12

Work-Life balance

"Balance" this word is so simple, no one needs a dictionary to understand the meaning of it, yet it is equally difficult to implement or have it in our lives.

Google Definition - Balance is a situation in which different elements are equal or in the correct proportion, enabling something or someone to remain straight and steady.

We start hearing this word from our childhood days and keep on hearing till we die.

During our childhood, our parents used to tell us to maintain a balance between our playing and study time. Most of our parents brought us up in such a way that these two elements are managed in a proportional way. So, we all know the meaning of balance, because it has been deeply rooted in us since our childhood.

As the definition says, to remain straight and steady, we need to have balance in life. Most of us acquire different personal and professional aspirations, these aspirations do not allow us remain balanced, straight and steady. To achieve those aspirations, most of us cannot keep ourselves steady and then lose our own identities. Some of us start focusing more on our personal goals so much so that we start compromising our professional lives, whereas others start focusing so much on professional goals that personal lives start getting impacted adversely, hence we are not able to remain steady in life.

We need to strike a balance in everything we do. Most times, we get so engrossed with our careers, jobs, or businesses that we compromise on our relationship with family, relationships with friends, and even relationship with ourselves. We concentrate so much on work to achieve our materialistic goals. Though it is not bad to worship our work, it should not be at the cost of our families, friends, our own peace, and our own identities because at the end, we do not enjoy life and forget who we are.

We should understand that it is essential that even as we make work important and it takes center stage, we must make time for our families, our friends and ourselves. If we do not do that, we will not be able to achieve our materialistic goals. Even if we achieve them, we will not be able to celebrate our achievements with our family and friends.

We believe that, to achieve our materialistic goals we have to really work and invest fully in that work, which is quite true and practical, but what we fail to realize is that when we do not strike a balance, in spite of achieving materialistic goals we do not get happiness. When we fail to take time out for our families, for our friends and for our own self, we become workaholics; we not only burn out fast, but because of that imbalance, we create distance from our families and friends.

We cannot be workaholics and remain consistent for a long time; we need to strike a balance between being a workaholic and having a personal life. If you do that, not only will you be able to achieve your materialistic goals, you will also achieve your personal goals CONSISTENTLY and not lose your identity.

So, when you move ahead in life, get into a business or any kind of career path and you really want to succeed, knowing competition is stiff, and feel you have to slug it out to be successful, trying hard to prove yourself, remember that you also need to take care of your personal life. Do not concentrate only on your work life, because the achievement of one should not be at the cost of the other.

There are a lot of people who have made a huge success in their work life but with their families, their children, and their spouses or with people, they are huge failures. You see that some of them, despite the millions they have or the huge investments they own, are still not happy with their personal lives. On the contrary, there are a lot of people who have done well in their personal lives but they have not been able to do well in their professional lives and are not even able to provide basic facilities to their families. Both situations are not good as one cannot be at the cost of the other, both have to go hand in hand.

It is always important that you strike a balance between your personal life and professional life. Frequently, we end up focusing more on our professional goals at the cost of our personal lives. There is no harm in having stretched professional goals, but when you only focus on them, you will end up taking shortcuts in life. You might be able to achieve the goals but you will not be able to sustain them. So focus on your deeds, focus on your work, come to work with complete dedication and achieve those goals while striking a balance in your personal life. Have time for yourself, your spouse and other family members, respect them, care for them, love them and give your time to them.

There have been times when I feel that I have not been able to do justice with my loved ones and even though I had achieved my materialistic goals in my late 30s and early 40s, I still feel I could have done better with myself, my family, my spouse and my friends. Can I go back and bring back those twenty years? No, I cannot. This is why it is important to strike a balance between your personal and professional life so you do not lose your identity.

I see people, who have been able to strike a very good balance between their personal and professional lives, to be happy. I see their contentment; whatever their goals and their achievements, they have been able to sustain it and they maintain it because they have been able to strike a balance. When you have been able to strike a balance, there is a buy-in from both sides; your family, your friends and children understand your work, and your colleagues and business associates understand you are a family man and both parties know you will not compromise with either.

Saying it might seem easy, but believe you me, it is not. Striking a balance between your personal life and work life is basically a science and an art - it takes you thinking and making a conscious efforts to achieve it. In your day to day life, you should know the key things that are important to you, that will enable you to be a successful professional. On the other side, you should also know the key things your spouse likes: what are his/her likes and dislikes, his or her favorite movies, favorite places and do not assume that just taking them out for a vacation once a year, to a foreign place is knowing them well. No, it is not. Although it will make them happy, the daily things you do to make your family happy is what matters the most. That is work-life balance.

I see corporates take fifteen to twenty days leave and then whisk their family off to a foreign country for holidays and they feel they have achieved work-life balance. Work life balance happens in your daily routine, your daily life not just going for a holiday for fifteen to twenty days in a year. You should be able to figure out the needs of your business and also figure needs of your family, spouse, and friends then strike a balance. Yes, the holiday is necessary for you to unwind and come back refreshed, but it still does not answer to work-life balance.

Studies have shown that people who have achieved work-life balance are happier people and they achieve a lot as in they get a lot done. They are successful at work and happy at home. The have found ways to achieve their optimum self in their personal and professional life. You too can achieve work life balance.

So spend time with your own self, it will help you know yourself better, play games with your children, go for an evening walk with your spouse, take your parents out for an evening walk, spend time with your siblings, eat at least one meal a day with your family, go on a picnic with your family and childhood friends, see your kids growing and enjoy the journey because the time gone will never come back. Strike a balance with your professional and personal goals by VOICING IT OUT to your family, Let them also know your professional goals, so that they are also part of your professional life and they do not see this as an outsider.

Most of you do not carry your families and friends along in your professional and personal journey. Let them know your dreams, aspirations, and things which trigger your happiness; let them be part of your journey. If you have a spouse who does not like to talk about work, then make it brief, make them know you are ok or speak to a best friend. You really cannot drive two separate vehicles at one go. Your profession and personal life should be in one vehicle so that you can drive your life's vehicle safely without any accident, reach your personal, professional destination in time and remain HAPPY!

"Don't kill yourself trying to keep the artificial you alive" - Rajeev Dua

Chapter 13

Let the child remain alive within you

The moment the word "child" comes to our minds, we observe a big smile grow on our faces.

It will be easy for us to get the answer to that question once we understand a child's characteristics. Let us start by describing the qualities of a child.

A child is carefree, cheerful, interesting, enchanting, innocent, happy, unbiased, generous, curious, adventurous, loving, fun-loving, willing to learn and unlearn etc. A child has got so many positive characteristics worth emulating.

Most often than not, all of us at one point of time would have said, "I wish I could relive my childhood days". If you go back down memory lane, you will find an answer to why you said so.

In the journey called life, we have somewhere lost our innocence in the pursuit of achieving our materialistic goals and looking at perfection in our deeds. We are no more carefree; we have lost our simplicity. With age, our curious natures has also got faded as if we know everything; we no longer have the learning attitude, our flexibility has been lost in the lanes where we grew from a child to an adult. The willingness to learn and unlearn is something which we do not practice anymore. We have lost most of a child's characteristics in our journey and now, when we look back at our life we want to relive our childhood days.

There is a saying which I quite agree with "Don't grow up, it's a trap!" Yes, it can be a trap, but how can we keep that child within us alive? I have listed a few things we can do:

1) Do not take your life too seriously; just go with the flow and enjoy your life.

2) Do not look for perfection in everything you do.

3) Mistakes are bound to happen; learn from them and move on. Do not stop experimenting due to the fear of mistakes or failure.

4) Do not be judgmental. We are being judged too.

5) Try to maintain the flexibility in your nature and always keep yourself eager to learn and unlearn.

6) Be selfish like a child because you will not be able to take care of others without caring for yourself.

7) Let that innocence remain alive within you.

8) Let that curious nature remain alive, it will help you break the monotony of life.

9) Continue to play a sport of your choice. It will help you keep that child alive within you.

10) Do not always say 'I know' dare to say 'I don't know'.

Kids are happy when they play and engage in sports because all sports are exercises, and when they exercise, their bodies release chemicals called endorphins. These chemicals trigger a positive feeling in the body, similar to that of morphine. That feeling, known as a "Runner's High," can be accompanied by a positive and energizing outlook on life. Now imagine being as happy as a child all the time.

You will also be disciplined because engaging in a sporting activity usually comes with a coach or instructor who will give you directions/guidelines. You can capitalise on your strengths and overcome your weaknesses. As you grow, these lessons learned during sporting activities become a part of you. When we keep the child within us alive, we will maintain and live a healthy life, mentally, emotionally and physically.

We know a child is carefree because they are not concerned with what people think if they do something wrong or right. They are not judgmental and the reason for this is because they know that if they tend to be judgmental they will get judged too. They do not have a fear of being critical and hence are not scared of being judged. They approach life with an open mind, a 'live and let live' attitude, whereas an adult changes his attitude, style of walking, and personality over time because he is afraid of being judged. An adult will question everything they do, without asking - 'Is this what I desire?' OR 'Does this please me?'

No, he questions or judges himself against the backdrop of - 'What will my friends say?' 'What will my family think?' 'Does society approve?'

As we grow older and become adults, as we move ahead in life, we forget that we were kids once upon a time. We forget the magic that the child within us is capable of creating. We allow the toils and spoils of life to dampen our childlike qualities as we get overwhelmed with responsibilities. We become victims of circumstances and situations; we become victims of relations, the environment, and so on. These factors will go on to shape and define our personalities as we transition from childhood to adulthood.

A life lived without paying attention to the child within us makes for a monotonous life; a life lacking in variety and interests; life becomes dull, tedious and repetitive. We find ourselves doing the same things, following the same routines daily, weekly, yearly - Oh what a bore!

Then one day we reach a certain age and think 'Oh my goodness, life was so good when I was young'. We find ourselves going down memory lane and recalling all the captivating and enchanting moments that were our childhood, we find ourselves craving all that childhood experience once again.

Yes, we are aware that change is the only constant thing and we cannot remain children permanently. Every child one day becomes an adult, and personalities need to take shape as we grow. We grow, get old and will one day exit the earth, this is a universal truth. With this fact at the back of our minds, why can we not purposefully ensure that we keep the child alive within us? That child that makes adult life interesting and fun!

We adults pretend that we know everything therefore we have the tendency to dictate to people what act of theirs is right or wrong, unaware that when we are judgmental of others we tend to fear the same trait in ourselves. Hence we are scared of being judged, and we tweak our original personality, cover it with layers of false character that is not originally ours, to suit what others say; indirectly seeking approval not from ourselves but family, friends, and society. This gives birth to a fake personality that seeks to make others apart from ourselves, happy.

As adults we can keep our inner child alive by engaging ourselves in sporting activities that we use to love or admire as children. When I was young, I use to play volleyball and I was the captain of my team. Till date when I see people playing volleyball, I cannot resist the urge to join them. I still love that sport and when I am playing, I get lost in the euphoria and I forget that I am the President, Vice president and Director of a company. I only immerse myself in the joy I derive from playing that game because that is what gives me a kick in life; that is my childhood love; that was my motivational tool as a child.

Therefore, by indulging yourself in sports, you still have the urge to win and understand how to manage defeats. When you are playing sports, you are detaching yourself from the routine of work and you are only concentrating on playing, which would mean enjoying yourself. So indulge yourself in a sport you really love or learn a new sport that you are keen on. When you do this, you will always be connected to your roots, you will always have that flexibility in you, your childlike qualities.

Another strong and beautiful quality of a child is their innocence. As we grow into adulthood, we lose that innocence, we lose that purity and genuineness in relationships; why can we not have that innocence in adulthood and purity in all our relations?

Also, a child is so flexible, one day he learns something new, perhaps from his favorite cartoon or a game and by the second day, if the same thing is not working well for him or he finds it unappealing, he changes his stance and unlearns that thing. He does not stay dwelling on something that has lost its appeal to him, he quickly relearns something new, and most times something that is relevant for that new day. So we should have that childlike flexibility in life.

Some of these negative attitudes come with the ownership mentality, not wanting to give up, not wanting to fail and it should not be so. Living childlike is being able to exhibit these qualities. If we live like a child, we will not live our lives the way we live now. We are not flexible, and we are unwilling to learn, unlearn and relearn. It is easy for us to put it out there to people that we have a learning attitude, and we are quick to learn and so on, but that is usually not the case. When learning something new, you should also learn how to unlearn it if and when they become irrelevant or the knowledge serves no other purpose.

Keeping the child alive within us enables us to stay connected to our roots, by remembering what we were as children, our strengths, our weaknesses and how to plunge further with no-holds-barred. When you stay connected to what you were in the early stage of life, you become aware of what motivates you, what makes you tick and gives you a kick in life, what you are passionate about, and become your own person.

You are in control of your world; you own your responsibilities and are able to fulfill them. You will keep yourself alive by having no regrets at the later stage of your life, you will not get lost in the journey called life, you will always be able to meet that child and you will not let go of his hand ever because after all, that child is YOU.

"Live to leave a legacy"
- Rajeev Dua

Chapter 14

Live to leave a legacy

Legacy is a gift or a carried forward property or asset that comes to you from your ancestors, parents, and elders. Most of us spend our lives enhancing our wealth, property, bank balance, and achieving our professional goals. We assume that our children, family members, friends, and society will remember us for all this when we are not there.

By the way, achieving and working towards materialistic goals is not bad, as long as we add value to the society and work towards the uplifting of poor and needy people. Working towards giving a good education to our kids is not bad as long as we are considerate towards poor people, those who do not even have access to basics like food and education. Making a good house for ourselves and our families is fine as long as we empathize with people who do not even have basic shelter. Enhancing your bank balance is not bad as long as it is not at the cost of your integrity and your value system.

Having said so, I am not expecting all of us to behave or live life like an NGO or a socialite, and keep all our materialistic goals aside. No, I am not saying that. Money is equally vital for us to do any kind of social work but earning money and creating wealth should not be the sole purpose of life; social work and earning money should go hand in hand.

In creating a legacy, we are not all required to carry out extensive expenditure projects like building an orphanage, hospital, or school. What is needed is our empathy and sympathy towards poor people. I also understand and appreciate that all of us cannot really build schools or colleges for underprivileged people, but we can undoubtedly find one child in a month to help buy school books for or pay the school fees. Many of us cannot build houses for poor people but we can certainly find a way to give shelter to poor people and help those in orphanages or old people's homes by contributing to such institutions, working towards uplifting the underprivileged. Thus, we are indeed building a legacy. Giving money to a roadside beggar is not considered social work, but working towards employing poor people to eradicate poverty is social work. It shall undoubtedly help you create your Legacy.

To me, LEGACY is the memory people have about you for your deeds, the remembrance of the work you did, your contribution to society, and the value system you gave to your children. All these can be materialistic or non-materialistic, but it should add value to someone else's life. If you are not adding value to someone's life and contributing only to your own wealth, confining it only to your own family, then that is not a legacy.

Just try and recall some people who have left a strong legacy behind like Mother Teressa, Mahatama Gandhi, Nelson Mandela, Dhirubhai Ambani, J.R.D Tata and Ratan Tata. Do we really remember them only for the wealth and assets they left behind or do we remember them for their contributions towards our society. Yes, we do not know the bank balance or assets of these people when they left this world, but we fondly remember them for the contributions they made to society and that is legacy to me.

We should be remembered for our deeds, our works and our

contributions to our society. No one will know our bank balance, the number of houses, farms and our exact wealth we own when we leave this earth, only our family will have this knowledge and maybe some of our very close friends. We will only be remembered by the society for the value that we added to them.

This is a mistake we easily make. We chase after money, materialistic goals, success and later in life, we find ourselves isolated and alone. This is because people who remained with us when we were young, were the people with materialistic desires, and since we did not work on non-materialistic things throughout our lives, at the later part we would find ourselves alone. Throughout our lives, we chased only money and did not create an ecosystem around us driven by social work, empathy and the upliftment of other people. In the later part of our lives we become irrelevant to the people around us because they do not see any further benefit coming from us to them.

On the contrary when we create an identity for ourselves with our social works and deeds to our society, then we will always be surrounded with people, irrespective of our age, also we will be remembered even after our lives are gone; that is legacy.

I would advise that we should not only run after money and positions, but also create value for the people around us. This is the legacy that will keep us alive in their hearts. So do not spend your life building only business and thinking about the gains and remuneration of what you have contributed, because life is not about all this alone. There is a lot of difference between life and business, but we spend all our lives like if it is a business venture. Thinking if I do this I will get this, that if I give more I will get more; that is not life. With that, you will be able to create wealth for yourself but not a legacy.

Most of us, when we start living our lives like a business venture, lose our core purpose of life in the entire process, and then we will realize this in the later part of our lives. By that time, it is too late. Very few people will remember you for your wealth but many acquainted and unacquainted people will love and respect you for the legacy you have left behind.

Chasing only your materialistic desires and creating wealth for you and your family will not create your legacy. Let us try not do that anymore. Money will fade one day but the legacy of your good deeds will never fade because when a legacy is strong, people will follow your legacy, people will follow your deeds and the more followers you have, the more your legacy will be sharpened. Your good work will get carried forward by your followers when you are not there and it will not fade.

The fact of life is that responsibilities shall always keep you busy and will never leave you. All of us have responsibilities and we live our lives with so many responsibilities which we think will build our legacy but it normally does not. We think that when we fulfill our responsibility towards our families, spouses, children, work and friends that we have created a legacy to be remembered for; that it will recall our influence on them but it would not be called as legacy.

When you become selfless, look at the society and ask what value you can offer to your society, then you can create a legacy for yourself. You cannot create legacy for someone else, you can only create a legacy for your own self. Look at your own strengths, the strengths that can add value to your society and pass on those strengths to others, so as to carry forward that work when you are not around.

When we came to this world, we saw it in a certain shape. It is our responsibility not only to leave it in a better state but to also leave a legacy (ways of working) that our children and others shall follow for further improvement of the world; one that will benefit our future generations.

"Consistently compromising with your own self will prevent you from sacrifice in the long run" - Rajeev Dua

Chapter 15

Sacrifice & Compromise

Sacrifice and compromise are two sides of one coin, but the meaning and the impact of each of them is different in our lives. Both are part of our daily lives; from our childhood days we sacrifice and compromise deliberately or unintentionally in our lives.

Let us understand the meaning of both words to measure their impact on our lives. Sacrifice is giving up something very important for someone very close to us, we feel contented in doing so, and there is no adverse impact on us. In comparison, compromise is giving up something very important to someone close to us at the cost of our happiness, comfort, and peace, and it also has an adverse impact on us. Often, we are not happy in taking such decisions but have to accept a lower standard to make someone else happy, which we would have not taken in normal circumstances.

In our endeavor to spread happiness and make our loved ones happy, we take a lot of decisions in the journey of life, some of them hurt us, and some of them do not. We do this to make our loved ones happy because we are emotionally attached to them.

There is no harm in giving up something for others, as long as it gives us happiness, and it is not at the cost of our peace, comfort, or joy and does not harm us.

We tend to take a lot of sacrificing and compromising decisions throughout our lives, which is how our lives go on. Both situations are inevitable in life, and neither is superior or inferior to the other, as they are two sides of the same coin, and we have to take both of the decisions in life. We cannot avoid any of them. The only thing is that we should know their impact on us and therewith, strike a balance.

In reality, we have to sacrifice a lot of things for our families and loved ones in the practical world, and we cannot be thinking about what we want all the time. However, while making these decisions, we must evaluate the impact of these decisions on ourselves. There is no harm in thinking about your own self and being a little selfish; I cannot say this enough. Be a little selfish for your own sake while taking some of these decisions.

Most of us do not understand the difference between these two and live our entire lives in this confusion. We live our whole lives making our friends and families happy, and in the course of it, we make a lot of compromises with ourselves. We generally confuse all these compromising acts with sacrifice. I call some of these acts compromises because some of the decisions would not have been taken if we did not consider our families' wellbeing. We usually agree to settle based on things that are not up to our expectations, and as a result, these decisions hurt us.

As long as we are aware of our decisions' implications and are considerate, not being repeated, despite knowing the adverse impact on us, it is okay. However, most of us take compromising decisions repeatedly, without analysing their impact on ourselves; or despite being aware, we take such decisions that have an adverse impact on us. Later in life, we repent and want to relive our past years.

Let me try to explain what I mean by compromise. Let us look at a young man who gained a scholarship to travel abroad and study in a prestigious school, he got this scholarship on his last attempt, which was his last chance to study abroad in a prestigious school. However, the young man had to give it up because his brother fell ill, and as he is the only brother, he had to stay back to look after him. Though, he needed that scholarship, he got it on his last attempt, and it was an opportunity for him to preserve his future and live a good life; however, he had to forgo his scholarship for his brother's wellbeing, while in truth, it will indeed have an adverse impact on his career, he had to compromise with his own life.

Now in that story, he gave up the promise of a brighter future, though he was happy with the decision he made it had a substantial adverse impact on his life. We are humans, surrounded by family and friends. We live in a society where we have to take such decisions and, while there is no harm in taking such decisions, we have to be mindful that such choices are not too frequent; otherwise, they will harm us, and we will repent in the later part of our lives.

Let me now try to explain what I mean by sacrifice; I decided to take up a new job in Nigeria when I left India. As a result of this decision, I had to leave my wonderful corporate life in India, my family, and friends behind. The impact of this decision was well evaluated, and I also knew that I was making this decision for four years to take care of my son's education and earn some spare money to secure mine and my family's future. Though I had to settle for something other than I long for (being with my family) It did not have any long-term adverse impact on me, and I was quite happy taking this decision because it was for my son's bright future. Therefore I call this decision of mine a sacrificing decision.

As long as you are aware that you are making a decision and know its impact, it is acceptable to make such decisions. However, many people amongst us live their entire lives only for others, while compromising on themselves without knowing the cost of their decision, they later regret not fulfilling their own dreams and desires.

In life, you need to understand the impact of the decisions you make and act accordingly. Striking a balance between sacrificial and compromising decisions is paramount; otherwise, you will lose yourself in this journey called life.

It is a fact of life that the people you are making the sacrifice or compromise for will not remain with you forever. The only person who will always stay with you is YOU; so do not take yourself for granted. Consider yourself before making any decisions in life. Evaluate the long and short-term implications of those decisions on you; you should not lose sight of yourself by living only for others.

If you live life only for your family, friends, and society, you will reach a point where those people are not around, and you are left alone. Later, you will realize that you have diluted your own identity by making so many compromising decisions, compromised with your health, desires, and happiness. Please remember, you do not have a rewind button in life, so your life cannot be reversed to take corrective actions. It is always good to evaluate your decisions, and make your life meaningful so that you do not repent later.

Evaluate all decisions, look at how they will affect you now and in the future; this is what we call self-care. Self-care literally means that you are mindful of your own needs, desires, and happiness, so that you are in the position to give appropriate support to your loved ones and the people who matter to you. So when you are thinking about your family, friends, colleagues, and society, think about yourself too. Think, 'In this decision, will I sacrifice or compromise, and when I do, how will it affect me now and in the future? Will I repent of it, or will I celebrate it? Will it infringe on my happiness and affect my body and soul for a long run?' Yes, you need to make some sacrifices, and yes, sometimes you need to make compromises too, however, you must understand the impact of those decisions, prepare for the consequences of it, and do not get surprised in the later part of your life.

You lose your identity when you take compromising decisions regularly without analyzing the impact of them on your life, especially when you cannot achieve your own goals later on. It is crucial that you do the self-care check to ensure that you are not making everybody happy at the cost of your happiness. You cannot make anyone happy if you yourself are not happy.

"Be the doctor of your life instead of the patient" - Rajeev Dua

Chapter 16

Behave like a doctor instead of a patient

You must have been surprised with the topic of this chapter. How can I become a doctor without a medical degree and how can I become a patient when I am not sick? What does this mean?

I am trying to say that there is a lot to learn from the doctors around us in our lives' routines. To understand better, let us know the characteristics of a doctor.

A doctor starts his interaction with a patient by showing concern towards the patient and then gives the patient a patient hearing. He starts his investigation by asking many open-ended questions like, what did you eat yesterday and how long did you sleep at night? How do you feel this morning? Is there any pain in the throat or soreness in the tongue? He will proceed to check the heartbeat with a stethoscope, examine the nerves and check the pulse rate. He suggests some pathology tests to the patient, after which he analyses the reports and at the end prescribes the medication and requests the patient to come in after a specific time for a follow-up session.

Let us now analyze how a patient behaves; when a person is sick he becomes restless, he panics, at times the patient is crying due to pain, he becomes uncomfortable and emotionally weak. He starts making emotional (heart) instead of logical (brain) decisions and he expects empathy and kindness.

Now, let us go back to our normal routine and analyze. Do we behave more like a doctor or do we behave like a patient would instead?

When he approaches a doctor, he is crying and in pains, the patient is sick and unhappy, and the patient laments to the doctor.

We also live our lives like that; we tend to behave like a patient. We always make a fuss when things do not go our way; we lament about it going wrong, saying "This is not what I expected". Or we complain that something did not live up to our expectations; we complain through pains or discomfort, we say the job is not giving us satisfaction, or the business is not giving us the desired results and happiness. We are not happy in our relationships; we are not happy with our spouses, our children are not doing well academically or otherwise, our relationships with our parents, friends, or relatives are not stable, and so on.

This is what we do; we live our lives filled with complaints and bitterness most of the time. We concentrate more on the negatives in our lives, dwelling on the unhappy moments in our lives, and focus more on our dissatisfaction rather than on the good, however little it may be.

In the journey of life, you will not always have ups, nor will you always be happy, there will be downs and unhappiness too. So, when you experience the low moments of life, when you are unhappy with the current situation in your life, always behave like a doctor. Ask yourself why it is happening. What could be the root cause? Remember, I started this chapter narrating what a doctor does when he meets a patient, I told you how he asks the patient open-ended questions, and the reason why he throws those open-ended questions to the patient is so he can get to the root cause of the patient's ailment.

Similarly, we should ask ourselves those open-ended questions. Talking to oneself is the biggest remedy because you know what exactly is wrong or right with you. The only thing that really stops us from doing this is that we are usually not honest with ourselves. If you are honest to yourself, believe me your life is going to be a beautiful and memorable one.

It is important you understand that no matter how good you are or how perfect you are, you will experience low and sad moments and that you may not always have perfect relationships with your parents, spouse, extended relatives, friends and colleagues. When this happens, ask open-ended questions like, why am I in this situation? What could be the root cause? Where did I go wrong? Where or how could I have done this better?

When you ask yourself these open-ended questions, and are honest with your answers, you will get the solution to whatever it is that ails you. If you can locate the root cause of a problem, then finding a solution is just one step away.

In your life also you should be a patient listener. Try and investigate the root cause of every situation, analyze the present and the future situation in conjunction with the past and present actions, take a mid-course correction (if required) based on your findings. Analyze your life's progress whether it is happening as per your interest, or if you have also become a victim of the rat race in the journey called life and finally, do a regular follow-up with your achievements/failures and see whether you know the reasons for both.

When you talk to yourself like a doctor would, you will ask

yourself genuine questions, and those genuine questions will be answered genuinely by you. So, in life when you have that kind of attitude, life will not give you room to lose your identity. When you have these questions in mind and you start behaving like a doctor, it means that you will always stay connected to your core strengths.

You know your likes and dislikes, and if for any reasons you find yourself being distracted from your values or your identity, then follow the same method. Behave like a doctor and ask open-ended questions till you get to the root of the problem, then make the necessary corrections. When you are able to make the corrections, it means you are on track and you will not lose your core identity, and your life will remain balanced.

You should understand that if somebody is behaving in a way, or a situation is happening below your expectations, there has to be a reason for it. So, instead of being judgmental or overly critical, behave like a doctor; get to the root cause of it, and find a solution. Stay connected to the person irrespective of the situation or circumstance; a doctor is always connected to a patient.

You should always stay connected like a doctor to the situations, circumstances, and core competencies you have. As you remain connected to them, you will be able to boldly welcome, face, and tackle challenges and problems.

A doctor is also courageous, and he does not think twice before deciding because if he has gotten to the root cause of the problem, his courage cannot waver; he will find the solution to his patient's pain. Be courageous in life; if you are courageous, you will find solutions to whatever problem you might be facing.

A doctor is also always optimistic; he is not pessimistic. So, you should always be optimistic in life, no matter the situation; do not be pessimistic at all. Desist from speaking negatively about your life, circumstances, or conditions. Avoid statements like, 'I know things are going to be tough. This will not happen. I know things are going to go against me' and so on. They are negative and should not be encouraged.

A doctor always goes about encouraging his patients with positive words like, "Hey brother, you are going to be fine; tomorrow is going to be better. Today you are better than you were yesterday". When the doctor makes these kinds of statements to the patient, the patient develops a positive mindset and is hopeful about his/her recovery.

You should also talk to yourselves with complete optimism; be optimistic about life generally. Pessimistic things do not leave a good impact on your life. All these characteristics of a doctor are what you should have within you, and when you do, you will not lose your core identity, you will not lose yourself in the cynical world or to negative or non-courageous people; you will be your true self.

When you behave like a patient and focus more on negative things like your failures, fears, dissatisfaction, and other harmful things in life, you will lose your core identity. This is because you will lose your confidence by concentrating more on your failures. By the way, illness is temporary, so are failures. So, you should focus more on your strengths and happy moments.

In life, when you start behaving like a doctor, emulating the positive things of a doctor, all these things will make you behave and live as your true self, and you will not get impacted negatively by challenges, nor will you lose your core identity.

"Happiness is not a destination; it's a journey"
- Rajeev Dua

Chapter 17

Am I really happy?

Surprisingly, the meaning of happiness is the same across all dictionaries. It is also the same in different languages. However, the essence of it varies from person to person.

In the journey called life, each individual gets exposed to different environments. The family construct of each individual is different. Each individual pursues different aims, taste varies from one to the other, challenges are different, priorities are different, circumstances and situations are different, and this is how our different individual personalities are. Hence the essence of happiness varies from person to person.

It is imperative that we know what true happiness means to us and how we can really experience it. Happiness is anything that brings a smile to anyone's face, including mine. It gives me inner pleasure, eases my tension, and makes me feel refreshed and it includes things and acts that give me a sense of achievement or satisfaction.

Many of us equate happiness with materialistic goals - like earning a lot of money, having a healthy social status, being famous, having a large house, owning a vast business empire, etc. Undoubtedly, all these materialistic things are important but can these things guarantee happiness? Are they capable of making us truly happy? I have my doubts.

Let me tell you, when I moved to Nigeria as a Director of a company, the position I assumed was the highest I had ever achieved in my entire professional career. Still, as far as my happiness was concerned, I could not say that I lived a very happy life. This is despite the fact that I had done reasonably well in my professional life. So, despite my fantastic earnings, a fancy designation, a respectable figure in the society, all these, I still did not have true "HAPPINESS."

 Now, I realize that I have compromised my happiness to achieve these professional gains, which I used to consider as happiness. So is there a real need to participate in such a never ending race which will also cost you your own happiness? Most often than not, we equate happiness with achieving materialistic desires, whereas the truth is they are achieved at the cost of our happiness.

The definition of happiness varies as it relates to different individuals, and often you find that people get confused defining happiness, pleasure, comfort and communion. They tend to consider these as happiness, those mentioned above could be sources of happiness but cannot be real happiness.

For me, what I have understood is that pleasure, comfort, and communion are temporary, while happiness is long-lasting. So, what is really important are those little things that give you comfort and convenience, yet we often tend to ignore these little things and take them for granted. We ignore the role they play in guaranteeing us long-lasting happiness.

For example, spending time with your spouse, playing with your children, eating food with your family, going on a long drive with your spouse, buying vegetables with your parents, or taking them for an evening walk while holding their hands. Consider also spending time with your childhood friends, going on a picnic with your siblings or close friends, just sitting aside and seeing your children grow and getting some free time to sit alone and to talk to yourself. All these acts appear to be normal, and you do them as routine; hence you take these small acts for granted, whereas they are the actual sources of happiness.

You should cherish these small acts because they will give you long-lasting happiness. Be it small or big, any routine activities that make you smile should be valued. Cherish them daily; once you do this, the comfort and conveniences will culminate into long-lasting happiness.

What is important is the consistency of happiness, which is missing amongst all of us. You are happy today, and maybe tomorrow or the day after, you get lost in participating in the race of achieving your materialistic desires; you forget why you were either happy or unhappy. You keep on doing those normal things, those daily routines that tend to drain you mentally, you ignore your mental health for the sake of your materialistic goals, and this is dangerous.

Maintaining the balance between physical and mental health is vital, and taking a pause, talking to your own self, sharing your success and failures with your loved ones, spending quality time with your family is the key to good mental health. It will lead you to happiness.

Maintaining the consistency of being in a state of happiness is what is really important in achieving long term happiness. Everyone should also understand the difference between achieving materialistic goals, achieving financial goals, achieving social goals, achieving family goals, etc. All these achievements will not give you happiness. Do not get confused about achieving those goals mentioned above and equating them with happiness.

Sometimes when you are at the peak, experiencing the best time of your life, when you have acquired a lot of wealth, reached an acclaimed social status. You have done well in your family; you find that even after all you have achieved, you are still unhappy, it dawns on you that you have not discovered true happiness.

Like I said earlier do not confuse or equate your ability to achieving set goals or acquiring material wealth with happiness. When you confuse your ability in achieving materialistic goals with happiness, more often than not, you compromise with your health; health is the true wealth. Still, most of the time you are running after comfort at the cost of your own health: If and when you are able to strike a balance between achieving them and maintaining a solid balance with your own health, peace, your friends, your society, your family, then you will discover and experience long-lasting happiness. So do not confuse happiness with your ability to achieve materialistic goals; there is no connection between them; they are worlds apart. One should understand that.

"Achieving materialistic goals can give you comfort but not happiness" – Rajeev Dua

Another example - When there was a survey conducted of the country with the happiest people, the United States of America with its best technology, top army strength, and solid financial capability, should have been considered number one globally. Still, when the survey was done in terms of the happiness index, the US placed seventeenth among other countries. This is despite their being number one in wealth, finance, technology and military strength. This goes to show that there is no correlation between material things and happiness as a state of being.

It means that happiness is an intangible thing; it is not something you can grab and hold in your hands or see. What it means is that you can feel it. It is not something that is your final destination; it is your way of life; it is the journey of your life, so your habits, lifestyle, or pattern of living should be so that you enjoy every moment you live. You should know what gives you happiness, discover them and when you do, cherish them. You should cherish those elements and be consistent in loving them. Being consistent is converting them into happiness. Value the smallest daily routine, which gives you satisfaction. So, happiness for me is a way of life; it is not a destination. Most times, people get confused and make happiness a destination because they chase something intangible. Their way of life is something they easily forget, so please do not focus on your destination instead of focusing on your journey. You will not be able to reach your destination if you do not concentrate on your journey.

- The journey of happiness.

"Obsolescence cannot be stopped; it can only be postponed" - Rajeev Dua

Chapter 18

Learn to unlearn, Unlearn to learn

Can we pour water into a cup that is already full? No, we cannot. If we need to fill the cup, we need to take some water from it to generate space for fresh water to come in. This is what we need to do with our lives as well.

There is an unnecessary load of experiences, education, learnings and grudges in our minds that occupy a lot of space and are not relevant for today's world. We are running our lives with that unnecessary load that is slowing our pace and creating obstacles for us in life. The sad thing is that most of us are not even aware of it. We need to take off this unnecessary load from our past, from our minds, to create fresh space for the new learnings that are actually relevant for today's world.

Today most of the mobile applications we are frequently using did not even exist in our school or college days. Most of what is being taught in school today might not be relevant tomorrow, and the chances are that things that would be relevant in the future do not even exist today. The world is so dynamic and is changing so fast. Therefore learning to unlearn and unlearning to learn is the need of the hour.

We spend our entire time learning, gaining skills, improving our competencies, acquiring new degrees and certificates, and expanding our knowledge base; this is how we grow and live our lives. Whatever we do, whoever we are, every day we learn and acquire new competencies. The decision to acquire this knowledge and certificates is either ours or as instructed by our elders.

Some of the things imparted to us are from the legacy of nature. Our elders inherited those skills or practices from their elders, so we are expected to inherit from them. Sometimes this impacts adversely on us. It is essential for us to periodically unlearn somethings that are not relevant in today's dynamic world. Unlearning is more important than learning; unlearning will help us let go of those skills that are not relevant to us anymore, the competencies and acquired knowledge that has become obsolete and no longer required.

Unlearning things that have become irrelevant leaves us free from baggage. It helps us let go of past experiences' baggage because, after a certain age and experience in the journey of life, we tend to carry a lot of baggage from our past. We begin to say 'I know everything,' 'I have done so much in life,' 'I have so many years of experience,' etc. This baggage is always with us, and we live with that baggage throughout our lives. The baggage becomes something we treat as an asset until it turns out to be a liability for all of us. It is not an asset anymore because those experiences which were once relevant to us at one point in our life is not relevant anymore. We need to recognize when something is no longer relevant. Ideally, it should be unlearnt and let go of entirely or perhaps, get upgraded and a different way found to make it suitable for the future.

Once we have the attitude of unlearning, it will allow us to remain flexible and receptive in life. This flexibility or receptive nature will allow us to remain rooted, empathetic, and logical, which is important in today's life.

Unlearning is a process where we either completely stop doing something or start doing something better or innovative. Unwittingly, unlearning leads us through a process of learning, which helps us to reinvent ourselves. Unlearning and learning are two sides of one coin, which always stay together and goes hand-in-hand.

In learning to unlearn and unlearning to learn, what we do is reinvent ourselves. To reinvent ourselves means to upgrade and make ourselves relevant for the future. It would mean we have to be introspective and have a good look at ourselves this way - yes, we have been successful professionals, successful parents or friends but there are some things, professionally or personally which are not really relevant anymore or which can be done differently to make it relevant again.

Skills and technology that made you successful in the past cannot guarantee your future success.

There was a time when people used to send handwritten letters. People used to write and send greeting cards via post, but these are no longer the popular means of communication. They have become obsolete, in some places, they are not in existence today. So, does it mean that people have stopped writing letters, sending postcards, or sending best wishes? No, people have not stopped. People still write letters and send greeting cards, but now all these are mainly done electronically, we write emails and even send electronic cards. If this means of communication was not reinvented, imagine the whole process of writing a letter, the need for physical delivery, and the period one had to wait for delivery which sometimes took weeks and months. It was such a lengthy process, but now due to reinvention, you just put your thoughts in a computer or your phone, press some buttons on your keyboard, and send your thoughts to your loved and dear ones within seconds.

Things would not have been easier and faster if we had not adopted the technology. If we had not reinvented ourselves from physically sending handwritten letters to using electronic emails and messages using our smart phones or computer, imagine what the future would have looked like.

Another example I like to state is the photo/picture industry. A few companies dealt with old model cameras with clicking pictures, but those old model cameras are gone now. It went from having a photographer take your pictures using a film strip, getting it washed in the studio room, before they are finally developed into pictures on paper, to what it is now. It was a lengthy and tedious process. With the innovation of new technology, everyone now has a digital camera in their mobile phones. People do not really need physical pictures anymore, so technology was reinvented.

Most mobile phone companies understood the need of the customer and captured the space of digital photography and the characteristic of being merely a talking instrument. In today's world, when people want to buy a handset, they look at its camera quality more than its ability to be used just as a talking instrument. Landlines are another example of what has gone extinct due to the consumer's need in this fast-paced world. Cell phones have replaced landlines because of convenience and speedy way of communication.

All of us must upgrade ourselves if we are to remain relevant both now and in the future. If we do not upgrade at the appropriate time, we will become obsolete and irrelevant one day.

Life is not static. Life is always evolving, changing every moment, and things that are relevant today might not be relevant tomorrow and vice versa. The universal truth is everything will get obsolete one day.

There are reasons why humans become obsolete. For example, humans become obsolete at the age of sixty when they retire, it might vary slightly from country to country but the average retirement age in the world is sixty. At sixty, you are expected to retire from employment; hence you become obsolete due to your age. Some people have to stop working due to health issues, so their health becomes the reason of their obsolescence. While for others, it is for lack of competencies and capabilities that they become obsolete. They are not competent to meet a job's requirement or do not have the competency to move to the next job level.

The fact is that we can never shy away from getting obsolete; we will surely get obsolete one day. Obsolescence can only be delayed or postponed depending on how efficiently we upgrade ourselves. Still, ultimately it is inevitable, and all of us shall become obsolete one day, and the ultimate reason for our obsolescence will be our own deaths.

Suppose we want to delay and postpone obsolesce. In that case, it is essential to keep upgrading ourselves and imbibe the unlearning skill. This will help us postpone obsolescence. When we do all this, we keep ourselves relevant not just for the present but also for the future.

We must always bear in mind that if we want to remain relevant for the future, we have to focus on unlearning and learning simultaneously and acquiring new skills and adapting new technology.

Upgrading yourself does not mean that you have to lose your own core identity. To upgrade is to make yourself relevant for the future without compromising your core strengths and core identity. You must upgrade yourselves from time to time. To reinvent yourself, you have to unlearn so that you can shed excess weight and baggage off to remain lean, move faster, and become a fast learner. You should remember your core strength and identity and do not compromise with them in reinventing yourself. You should not become victims of acquiring skills; your up-grading should not be at the cost of your own identity. You should not be copying things which you yourselves are not good at.

"Learning doesn't happen without unlearning, and unlearning fastens the process of learning" – Rajeev Dua.

"GURU - Guides U and Restricts
U from moving in the wrong
direction" - Rajeev Dua

Chapter 19

Having a mentor is very important in life

Have you ever observed a difference in how you talk to someone junior or younger compared to when you talk to someone older or senior to you?

When you talk to your elder or senior, you are mostly respectful, receptive and humble; on the contrary, you behave a little more authoritative and directive when you talk to your junior or someone younger. Why do you behave differently with different sets of people?

As we live our lives, create an identity worth applauding, for most of us, our success forces us to lose our humility. We begin to feel better than others, and we look down on others, we think no one is better than us like we know everything, we become a little arrogant and lose our empathy towards people. We develop these negative traits in our behavior because our success forces us to feel better than others. This is a natural thing, but it should not happen at the cost of our humility.

How do we continue to do well yet remain humble?

If you have someone who you look up to or treat as a mentor, coach or teacher, it basically gives you a sense of being a student with a feeling at the back of mind that you are always learning.

You will always have some kind of confidence that someone is available to upgrade, guide, and coach you. This thought will keep you conscious that you are still a student and learning each day; this will always allow you to remain humble throughout life.

Your coach, teacher or mentor does not allow you to be arrogant towards your juniors. It makes the student remain alive within you, keeping your learning and unlearning ability active within you. It keeps your competitive spirit alive, improves your listening skills, preserves your empathy intact, stops you from being judgmental and last but not the least, keeps you humble. Humility is so important in life. It is an attribute and virtue everyone should aspire to possess. Most often, when you do not have a mentor, teacher and a coach you forget these basic attributes of living.

Having a coach or mentor will enable you to live a healthy and fruitful life. I am a successful professional, I have a fantastic family life, and because of this, I get carried away and become a little arrogant, both at work and home. This is because of my human nature. However, I have a spiritual guru who I take spiritual advice from. He guides me through my spiritual needs, and it eventually helps me in my personal and professional life.

My spiritual teacher (Guru) understands me as a person, takes care of my spiritual needs, and guides me towards being a better human. Whenever I feel I am treading on the wrong path, I am disturbed in anyway, not mentally satisfied, my spirits are down or I am indecisive about something, I look up to my teacher, I seek him out for guidance.

When and how I speak to my spiritual guru is a lot different from how I speak to others and the discussions are different. When I talk to him I am incredibly polite, even when I remember him, irrespective of his absence. I completely surrender myself to him as if I do not know anything. I am like a child before my spiritual teacher, and he guides me, understands my problems, and listens to me patiently as I relate my situation to him. In doing this, I am relieved of whatever is stressing me at that moment. I dump whatever has been weighing me down to him, relieve my heart of that burden and he gives me some direction and guidance. I have totally dedicated myself to him; this is not how I normally behave with other people.

Having a guru gives you a kind of psychological comfort, that if you lose your way in the journey called life, you have someone who will hold your hand to guide you back to the right path.

The presence of a coach, teacher or mentor in your life gives a certain kind of confidence that there is someone who will take care of you and that you are not entirely alone in life's struggle. You become mentally empowered and encouraged to take risks in life. You become clear of your goals and become positive, aggressive, and determined to pursue your goals because you know there is someone to guide and coach you.

Many characteristics are enhanced in you when you have a mentor, a teacher or a coach in your life. As I have stated earlier, humility is one of the characteristics that having a mentor or teacher in your life improves. Arrogance will not be found in your personality, and you will also be receptive to thoughts, ideas and opinions that differ from yours. You will not feel like you have a monopoly on knowledge, like you alone know everything in life, which is impossible. You will not boast that you have acquired all learning, and there is nothing new for you to learn. You will always be eager to learn, and you will still see yourself as a student and be willing to grasp whatever you are taught.

Your coach, mentor, or guru can also be younger than you. We make them our idols not because of their age or experience but because of their knowledge, which can influence and add value to our lives personally, professionally and spiritually.

When you have a coach, teacher, or mentor in your life, you will always be respectful, and you will be able to see people for who they are and still respect them - you will have respect both for the elderly and young. These characteristics will always remain in you when you have a coach in your life.

There is no age limit for being either a mentee or a mentor. You can become a mentee at the age of seventy, and you can also become a mentor at the age of twenty. If someone is able to add value to your personal, professional and spiritual life then he can be deemed as a teacher or mentor.

A coach knows your personal and/or professional strengths and weaknesses and he also knows you as a person. In the journey called life, when you exceed materialistic and social goals, you tend to lose your focus on your basics and gradually start losing your own identity and uniqueness. When you start doing things which are really not needed to maintain your so-called social status and ultimately move in the wrong direction, your guru is the one who keeps a check on you and ensures that you are on the right track and do not lose yourself in the journey called life.

"The worst can sometimes be the best; stay positive" - Rajeev Dua

Chapter 20

The worst can sometimes be the best

Someone has said, "No pain, no gain," and that is quite true. Every pain that we go through teaches us some lessons that help us live a happy life. The most important part is to know how to bear and handle that pain. Most of us cannot handle those tough times; therefore, we surrender to the adverse situation, lose our own identities, and shift our focus and direction elsewhere.

There is no pain as painful or as intense and excruciating as a woman giving birth to a baby. This is the highest pain any human can tolerate. This pain starts with the changes the lady experiences during the nine months she carries the baby in her womb. The lady observes a lot of physical and hormonal changes during those nine months, she observes changes even in her feeding habits amongst other but she will not mind because of the hope of carrying the baby; the thought of what it is all for is a lot to look forward to. She knows that once she holds her baby in her arms, everything will be fine. The hope of carrying the baby in her arms makes those painful nine months worth it.

Do you remember our early childhood days? When we were sent to school, we used to cry, and sometimes, some of our parents would cry along with us as they left us behind. It was not easy for either of us. As kids, we were not aware that this was being done to secure our future, but our parents were aware that today's pain and sorrow will eventually lead to a bright future.

When my son was three and half years old, we sent him to school for the first time. He cried so much during the first two or three weeks, and his tears deeply touched us that we did not want him to go back to school. We felt it so deeply that sometimes we used to go to the school to check on him and even sit with him in the class. I am sure you experienced this too.

However, that three and a half-year-old child is now studying engineering in the United States. Imagine if we had not let him go through that pain and stopped him when he was crying and refusing to go to school, imagine what he would have been today. He sure would not be what he is today.

So this is what life is all about. Life is like labour pains; you have to go through pains to achieve happiness. Sometimes we get into situations that we do not want to be in. There have been times in our personal and professional lives that we encountered unfavourable moments and problems. We saw no silver lining or life beyond them; we only saw gloomy weather and our approach towards life became negative. However, once we were out of that situation, we felt relaxed, and it gave us a lot of lessons for the future, to live our lives in a better manner.

One should always remember that adverse situations and tough times do not last forever. When we are in the midst of the situations, we may feel that this will never end, like it will last forever. We have all those negative thoughts coming into our minds but let me assure you, those days will go by, and things will fall into place. Then you will start to wonder how you survived that disaster, how you made it through. This, however, is the time to think through the lessons learned, because as I have come to realize from experience, those periods of life teach you things, a lot of lessons to help you foster forward.

For instance, leaving my comfort zone way back in my home town in India to come work in Nigeria, staying without my family and earn in dollars was not something I dreamt of happening when I was younger. Just like I never thought about becoming a family man but look at where I am today. I am earning good pay but it was not an easy decision. It was a tough one as I never realized how painful it will be to be far away from my family, my wife, my parents and my friends. It was exciting at first, but getting to Nigeria and staying for a while dawned on me and the pain gradually kicked in. However, I knew the pain was for the greater good, and I learned my lessons well. I could easily manage my financial responsibilities after coming to Nigeria.

Moreover, I could pursue my dream of writing this book after thinking of writing this book for almost five years. I could not do so in India, but Nigeria made it possible for me. So, always remember there is always a bright shinny sun after every dark night.

It has been almost two years now, and this period has taught me a lot of lessons. It has taught and made me understand my relationship with myself, now I know myself better than I knew before. I have also understood my relationship with my family and friends. It has taught me the importance of family and the role of friends in life. It has also taught me to understand the difference between friends and acquaintances.

The Nigeria tenure has opened my eyes to many things. We should not be taking things for granted in life, but value each and every thing in life, no matter how small or big it is - this I think I have learned after staying in this country. Nigeria has taught me to be persistent no matter the circumstances and focus on my ultimate goal, without looking at the adverse situations.

Talking to yourself at least once a day, seeing your spouse, parents, children, and friends every day is a blessing. Going out for a short drive or a dinner with your family, spending time with your parents for a cup of tea, going on a casual walk with your spouse, meeting your friends every week; these things looked so basic and elementary to me, till the time I left India. I took them for granted, but now that I am far away from family and friends, I understand their importance and miss them. So cherish every small activity you do in your daily life, as this is real happiness.

I am a family man, and I love being around my family. I am also a socialite, I love being in groups. I cannot stay alone, but for two years now, I have been alone, and it taught me that life here on is not going to be like my previous 45 years; it will not even be like the last year. Some people will still be here for me, and some will not.

To manage my loneliness, I picked up a hobby; I started writing a book that will be valuable to you and society. I also started listening to music, I had never cooked in my life but I started cooking like a professional chef. I used to consider such things as minor and never indulged in them but today, look at me, indulging and enjoying it.

Do not dwell much on unfavorable times, instead try and find a way out. If you cannot, use that time to learn something that can be of value to you or others. Always remember that time wasted during unfavorable circumstances can be used to learn something of value. I had never experienced or tried meditation, till I got in touch with the Art of Living Foundation and started my meditation sessions which I would say is one of the best things that happened to me. This not only distracted my mind from my adverse situation but also helped me live my life in a better manner.

So your tough times will teach you the best lessons to help you forge ahead. During this period the best thing is to write down all the lessons you are learning. You do not have to literally write, writing also means that to have it at the back of your mind. Later when you encounter similar situations, you will be able to manage it better, and you will not lose your identity to that tough circumstance.

I want you to take from my experience that I did not wallow during my tough times, but used it to do something of value. So when you are in a tight spot, do not much dwell in it and waste time, spend it doing something of value. It does not really matter how long you will pass through that situation, what will matter is the lessons you learnt and things you did to manage the situation.

People fall into depression because of how hard they take situations when they are not favorable to them. They feel lost and believe there is no remedy. They even go as far as thinking God cannot get them out of it. This is because they spend time over thinking about the issue instead of finding something of value to do while that time lasts. Always remember that tough times do not last forever, and they always teach you some lessons that will propel you to another angle, another victory and another success story.

To be exact and very precise, at this moment (21st Jan, 2021 13:30, Lagos), I am working from home due to the high number of cases of Covid -19 in the city. In fact, three colleagues living on the same premises with me had tested positive earlier; unfortunately, two of them have tested positive again today after staying quarantined for fifteen days. Imagine the pressure they would be going through. I am deeply concerned about them, and honestly, I was also stressed about my safety. So, I had the option of staying alone at home, dwelling on the impact of Covid-19, and getting into a negative state of mind. Or, taking the situation head-on, indulging myself in something that gives me happiness and makes me feel relaxed. I opted for the latter and decided to indulge myself in completing the twentieth chapter of my book. I listened to melodious songs and gave myself a treat by cooking masala rice along with mint sauce and yogurt. Believe me, I am enjoying this moment, and I have zero fear of Covid-19.

If it is your first time in such a situation, do not let it have the best of you; write down the lessons you are learning, just that alone is therapeutic and will help you pull through. In the future, if such an adverse circumstance rears its head again, the lessons written down will help you tackle the issue. Do not let it disturb you; do not let it have the best of you. Do not lose your identity in such situations. Find your three best characteristics during this situation and harness them because bad conditions make you a better person.

My exposure to the jewelry business (courtesy of Raghav Khandelwal and Kamal Agarwal), has taught me that the raw diamond is dirty and filled with impurities. It therefore has to pass through various polishing levels to gain its sparkle, shape, and structure, before it is crafted into a beautiful, sparkling necklace. If someone goes through the tough process of making a necklace, I bet they cannot even imagine that the piece which looks dirty and filthy today will eventually take the shape of a beautiful necklace tomorrow.

In life, we should not lose patience when we are passing through tough times. I am sure we will come out sparkling like a beautiful necklace once we patiently manage our tough times. We should understand that tough times are our refining period and that we are going to look beautiful and luxurious once we get out of that situation. We will come out with many learnings and lessons that will make us stronger and better in our professional and personal lives. Do not surrender yourself to adverse situations and lose your own identity rather face it like a warrior.

"Let 'the reel' you face 'the real' you,
at least once a day" - Rajeev Dua

Chapter 21

Real vs Reel

Reel is scripted, whereas real is actual.

REEL means a movie or a theatre act, which is mostly not reality. It is a fictitious story told for entertainment and is temporary, while REAL is actual, true to life. Reel life is artificial life, sometimes it can be close to real life but mostly it is not.

As we grow, most of us, if not all, start comparing ourselves with our siblings, friends, neighbors, and peers. We start comparing ourselves with others to look better than them; we start living to win over them, earn better, satisfy them, compete, dominate, and have the upper hand over them; in the process, we tend to forget who the 'real' us is.

We forget our own strengths, values, paths, likes and dislikes; thus, we lose our own identities. We start following the paths of others without even looking at our and resources, as a result, in the latter part of our lives, we blame ourselves for not being content, and happy, and we blame ourselves for missing out on our own goals.

Let us look at an imaginary situation where you are standing at a bus stop without knowing where to go. So you will remain at the bus stop in absence of the knowledge of where to go. Now, you imagine a situation where you know that you have to go to your own house, but instead of taking a bus going there, you take a bus going somewhere else. If you do so, will you be able to reach your own house? The answer is no. The reality is, if you have to go to your house, then you need to catch a bus going towards your own house, so that you can reach your destination.

Most of us behave as narrated in the example above. We do not know our own goals. Some of us choose the route of going towards someone else's goal without even looking at our capabilities, and few of us, despite knowing our personal goals, select the path that is not in line with our own goals; thus, we get lost. If we start chasing our goals while walking down someone else's path, we will not reach our destination. We will get lost in the journey, and we will use all the wrong methods and means to achieve our goals, which may not happen still because we have chosen the incorrect path. In this process, the Real you is lost, and the fictitious life of Reel you begins.

The reality of life is that we cannot choose somethings, like our parents; similarly, they did not get the chance to choose us, so we did not get the opportunity to choose our siblings. We have to remain satisfied and content with life.

There are a few things that are not in our control, but in life, our greed gets more profound with each passing day; hence we never get satisfied. As a result we lose focus on our goals, forget ourselves and start living a Reel life. So, focus and evaluate your own strengths and act accordingly.

To balance our real and reel life is to understand when to drop one and pick up the other. Let us use a party to explain what I am trying to say. Most of us (if not all) when we go out for a party, put on our fancy shoes, dress up just to look beautiful or handsome, put on a lot of makeup because there is a kind of competition to look better among the society. When the party is over, and we are back home from the party, the first thing we do is to remove the artificial makeover, the shoes, the dresses, and the make-up, because that is not a comfortable situation to be in, we all want to be at ease when we are back home.

This is what we should do too in our real lives. One should wear make-up once in a while; one should also know how much to put-on, and when to wipe it off. Makeup should be put on our face in such a way that it does not spoil our own skin and original beauty. We live our lives by putting on too much makeup (living the reel life) to look more beautiful or better, and as a result, we spoil our own selves. When we want to wipe-off that make-up and live a real life at the later stage of life, it is too late and then we regret wasting our entire lives, living a reel or artificial life.

We ruin ourselves spiritually and physically when we pay more attention to the reel life at the expense of the real life. So it is important to remove the fake make-up from our lives and let our real selves breathe, so that we do not contaminate our bodies and souls.

You play so many roles in your life. You should always keep one role alive within you, which is true to you; in a day, a week, a month, spend some time with yourself, only for you. Leave aside all your other roles and just concentrate on just YOU. Try to recall your childhood memories, when you were allowed to be yourself, remember those activities, moments, which made you happy, try remembering your own strengths: when you do this, you will not lose yourself in the journey called life. This is how the reel you will not be able to dominate the real YOU.

Once you start talking to yourself, ask yourself relevant; questions that will trigger your actions. Ask yourself if the action you are about to take for another role is required or not, and to what extent do you need to give the work so that it will not dominate you as a person and make you lose your own identity.

Sometimes, people have to live the reel life due to some compulsions of life; there is no harm living like that as long as it is not harming anyone, providing it is not done to portray yourself better than others. In all, the important thing is to know when to stop living the reel life and start living the real life.

Play on your core strengths, be aware of your likes and dislikes; know what really makes you happy, what gives you pleasure, and your capabilities and keep the learning attitude alive. Know your materialistic / non-materialistic desires and what you think they mean to you. Figure out why you really want them and ensure you are not attracted to them because your friends, family members or someone you know, has those things. You should have your to-do list based on your own abilities and requirements, not just to portray yourself as better than your peers. Rather, talk and compete with yourself every day, enhance your capabilities, raise your own bar to keep your competitiveness alive.

"We will not be able to achieve our own goals while chasing someone else's path" – Rajeev Dua

Another way to connect with the real you is to keep your close friends around you; they really know you as a person and vice versa. They are a constant reminder of your strengths, weaknesses, and your source of happiness. If the daily routine your life becomes so monotonous that everything looks normal to you, you do not see any need for improvement, you start flowing with the tide; these are the times when those close friends can help you break the monotony. They help your real-life remain alive and help you maintain a balance between both of them.

The real you gets converted into reel you when you start comparing yourself with others and want to be superior to others without considering your own strengths and capabilities. When you keep comparing yourself with others, you will never get satisfied because, by the time you reach their level, they will have raised their standard further and again, you start chasing to reach up to their level, a cycle that continues forever. As a result, in later parts of your life, you cannot achieve your own goals because you never chased them; instead you spend your entire life pursuing others. This is how you lose yourself in the journey called life.

"Make "the real" you so strong that it becomes "the reel" for others." – Rajeev Dua

**"There is no point in repenting
later if you have the opportunity to
correct it now" - Rajeev Dua**

Chapter 22

Live as if you have last five years to live

When I self-evaluate and see who I am - a reasonably accomplished corporate manager with twenty-three years of work experience who has a beautiful family (a wonderful son and beautiful wife, the best dad, and lovely friends)- it gives me a sense of immense satisfaction and makes me really happy.

 I am happy about my achievements, but I have not yet reached where I should have been. I still have milestones to reach, goals to achieve, and these are part of life, which is fine. We all strive for more, and when we get that more, we push the goal post even further. This is how life moves on.

For instance, as a student, when you study, you focus on being the top student in your class, and your focus will be to achieve this goal. When you pass, you move on to college, and the hustle begins as college is where our lives really take shape, for we learn all the good and evil over there. We usually start off in college from the age of eighteen or nineteen, so by the time we are in our early twenties, we are done with college and aspire to do more. Some of us go for further studies while some of us start our professional careers.

When we kick-start our careers, as it is our first time working and earning money, it gives us a lot of independence and gives us a sense of responsibility, but again we seek more. We always aspire to do our best to remain at the top in this competitive world.

Later, when we are professionally stable, we get into the commitment of life that is marriage. We start a family of our own, and create an extension of the family we came from. Now our priorities begin to change. We start thinking of new goals, making a better life for our families, and as such, we get engrossed with more materialistic goals; this is how life moves on - this is how I have passed my forty-five years of life.

A question came to my mind - Will I continue doing the same set of things and live my life the way I have been living it if I had five years left to live?

You must be wondering why five years? Instead of three, two, or one year? Or you must have heard people saying, "Live as if you have one day to live," etc. To me, five years is reasonable enough time to take correction (if any) in making short-term or long term decisions.

I pondered over this question for a few days and concluded that I could not continue to live the same way I had been living my life if these were my last five years to live. Why is it that despite being so successful and happy with my life, I would not want to continue to live the life I have been living all these years?

After thinking about it a lot, I realized that we run after money, run after accomplishments, run after social status, and run after success. These are materialistic goals. Yes, money can get things that can make you happy, but what is the essence of money if it cannot bring happiness to your life?

It is important that you understand that there is no correlation between money and happiness. If you have five years left to live and after evaluating, concluded that whatever you are doing today, you will discontinue right away to do something else, then my friend, that means you are not living your life the way you should have lived it.

Assume you have five years left to live; this thought in itself will make you push off a lot of professional and personal things that you may have been postponing or were not taking seriously. You are either concentrating more on your professional or personal life, at the expense of the other. Both situations are not acceptable.

If you need to look at your life in a balanced manner, try assuming it is the last five years of your life, and you will think about what you need to do; you will balance your life. You will balance your day-to-day activities, spend some time on your profession, and spend some more time with your family, friends, and a lot of time with yourself to do things that give you happiness.

It is a great way to evaluate your life and bring some balance to it. It will expose your sins and things you took for granted while chasing materialistic goals. It will make you realize where you lack in your family and with your spouse, things you failed to do, things you overlooked and left undone through the years chasing materialistic goals. It will help you see things in a new light and help you balance them.

Look at YOURSELF first; what gave you happiness when you were young? Remember those hobbies that made you happy, remember the things you were good at during your early days. Remind yourself of what YOU are aside from your family, friends, profession, and society. Start living life for yourself, do things that give you happiness rather than living for others. Start living your life NOW.

Look at your spouse, who is the largest, direct, and indirect contributor to your success. Most of the time, you take her/him for granted, considering that their contribution is his /her duty, and do not applaud them for their respective contributions. A few examples are making your breakfast, having lunch and dinner on time every day, taking the kids to school every day, and taking care of your parents whenever they need it. Your spouse also manages your social life because you are always busy with your work, pays off your credit cards bills, pays the kids school fees, and organizes your routine monthly expenditures. We take all this everyday work for granted; we never value the effort and keep moving ahead in life without thanking them for their contributions.

Make sure to recall all the smallest contributions you make to each other. Thank, appreciate, respect, and seek an apology (if required) from each other for your respective deeds, sacrifices and compromises. List out your couple's goals and try to achieve them together because there is no point achieving your couple's goals alone when either of you is not there; as no one knows who will leave before the other, do it NOW.

Look at your children, what are the things you will like to do with them that you have not done, and list down the things they have been yearning to do with you that work-life did not permit you to give from your time. You know children do not forget, so take time and work out what you will like to do with them before they grow up. They will not remain toddlers for so long, you know, they will not be children for so long. Make a decision today to list out all you would like to do with them and make sure you do them NOW.

Look at your friends; some of them would be your childhood friends, some of them would have met you during your early professional days, or some would have met you while socializing in society. Not all, but a few of them would have made a lasting impression on you, which has gotten a little faded due to your busy schedule. Go back to those friends, thank them for their contributions to your life and give them a big HUG. Do it NOW.

Think about your parents too; your parents taught you almost everything you knew as a kid. They raised you and have a vital role to play in the success you are now enjoying. There is no way you can repay your parents for their contributions to your life, but are we really acknowledging our parents' contribution by giving them adequate time and respect as they truly deserve? Start spending time with your parents, hold their hands, take them out for a walk the way they used to hold yours when you were a toddler, take care of their emotional and monetary needs because you never know when will be the last day for them. Do it NOW.

It is important to look at how you would like to live the last five years of your life. Make a list of things that give you happiness, because my friend, you never really know when the last day of your life will be; no one knows. So act upon it, correct your lifestyle before it is too late, list down those things you will like to do for yourself, your family, and your friends to give YOU happiness. There is no point in repenting later if you have an option to correct it now. So do it NOW.

You might list down some materialistic goals, like building a house, buying a car, traveling to an exotic island or whatever thing will give you happiness. Make sure they tie down to the last five years of your life; you will realize that you have not done a few important things for YOURSELF. These things you had always wanted to do for yourself, but somehow your personal and professional priorities have taken over you and your OWN preferences. You will realize you have been living for people, success, friends, and society, leaving YOU aside.

I think about how I spent so much time in this materialistic world, thinking and building, material things. I had materialistic goals, I thought of building a small house, which I did. I then thought of selling that house and buying another, and I did that too. I thought of one investment, two investments, and then more investments, and I continued. As I achieved one, I aimed for another now, I am forty-five, and I am thinking, when will I make a home? There is a difference between a house and a home. I have purchased many properties, but they are all properties. What I long for is a home, a small home, not a house. A house is made of concrete walls but emotions, love, and togetherness make a home for all family members.

Live your life as if you have just five years to live. If you evaluate and see that you do not have to change anything much from what you are presently doing, that is good. If you think you need some tweaking, then, by all means, tweak your life and make it more meaningful. By doing this and taking small steps to change it, you will live a happier life, you will be fulfilled and have no form of dissatisfaction, and you will not spend time regretting it. Most of us fall into the trap of life, hiding somewhere behind our materialistic goals and starting to find ourselves later in life, but it is too late by that time. Turn your life around and start living a life that gives happiness to YOU.

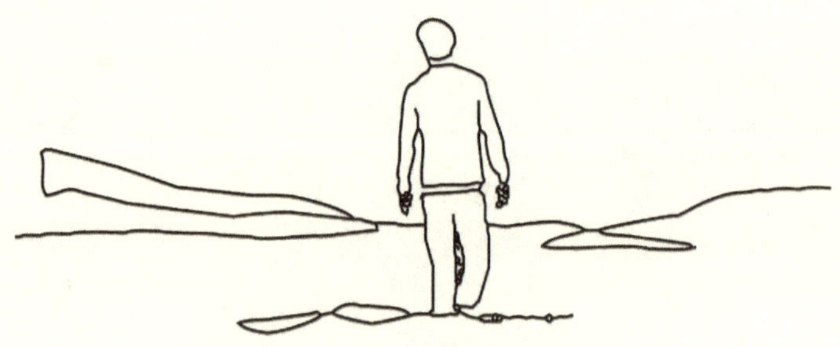

"Always remember, the one person who will never let you feel lonely is 'YOU' - Rajeev Dua

Chapter 23

Alone vs Lonely

There is a difference between being alone and being lonely.

Being alone is a physical attribute that can arise due to your choices or circumstances, whereas you do not choose loneliness; your mind is making you feel lonely. There are times when though many people surround you, you still feel lonely, whereas there are times when you are alone, yet you do not feel lonely.

Therefore it is fair to say that loneliness is a mental and emotional attribute while being alone is a physical attribute.

Loneliness is not so disturbing or alarming as we experience loneliness daily. We do not usually notice it because we have become accustomed to it. For instance, on our first day in preschool, our parents left us in the school by ourselves. Were we not left alone, and we felt lonely?

It happens all over again when we are through with primary school, to which we had gotten accustomed. We made friends with like-minded children and got to form relationships with our teachers and other people in the school. Then we graduated, and it happened all over again as we entered high school. This time we are about eleven or twelve years old and the school might be bigger, and we do not know anyone, probably because our friends from primary school are not in that school, our parents are not there also. In the first few days we stay alone, we again feel lonely, and then we make new friends and start bonding with the school as we find children with the same hobbies or like minds.

After a couple of years, we again graduate and go to college; then the circle repeats itself until we find a way to kill the loneliness by making friends and bonding with people. It happens again after we finish college and take on our first job. This time we are entirely on our own and full of expectations as we do not know what the job is really about or who the boss or colleagues are.

Even if it is your own business, you do not know where to kick off or which way the company will go. The loneliness sets in firmly as you do not know the people around you, and they have huge expectations of you.

For a limited time, you are lonely, you feel out of place, manage time, find ways and means to break that loneliness since you know that the people around you are hopeful and have to deliver. You try to prove your equity so that you improve your life and grow.

Loneliness also sets in when you are about to marry or are married and go to your in-laws' house for the first time. Though many people surround you, you feel lonely because you do not really know your spouse's parents and family, but with time, you start to get to know each other, bond with each other and relax. You start understanding them, and they start understanding you too.

In-between times there will be more bursts of loneliness, but you will find ways to manage them. You will then have kids who will grow and leave for college, and because you want them to be better people, you let them go, and then you will be alone again. The loneliness traps you because your mind will make you feel lonely, but you will find ways and means to manage it - to break the loneliness because there is an excellent possibility your kids will grow from there, marry and never come back home.

So you learn to manage things; learn to manage loneliness. However, loneliness is not always the same as being alone. As explained earlier, being alone can be a choice, so you can be happy and crave no physical presence around you, unlike in loneliness, where you are unhappy because you are not mentally happy and engaged.

Sometimes that physical presence is our parents. We find them sometimes living with us when they are old, and we love having them around, but the inevitable will happen someday as they have to leave us to be with God. Then we will be left alone again, and then the memories of their love will make us feel lonely without them, but we have to manage that too. We once again find a way or means to curb the loneliness. That is the reality.

So, in all the situations narrated above, we were surrounded by people in all different life stages; however, we still felt lonely because loneliness is a mental state, not a physical attribute.

Life teaches us how to manage these seasons of loneliness. Our parents, teachers, and the things around us have led us to manage these situations to an extent, to expect them, and live with them. Loneliness is a reality, and we must learn how to manage it since it is inevitable in the pyramid of life.

I have met people who could not cope with loneliness, and it shifted their focus from their purpose in life, from their goals, and their visions. Loneliness distracted them, and they started doing what they were not supposed to do as the loneliness led them towards other unpleasant and undesired paths. It is essential that we understand loneliness and how to manage it.

It is important because as we grow along our career paths, from a junior executive to a manager and then to a senior manager to executive then top executive, or while we develop our businesses, the loneliness will get stronger. It will increase as we move up the ladder of life. We know that we must grow in life, as growth is important and significant in life, and as we grow, we know that loneliness deepens as it grows with us, so we must learn how to manage loneliness to our benefit and growth.

As we grow from our childhood to adulthood and lust after materialistic goals, one of the things we neglect on the way is us. This is the mistake we usually make, as I have noticed it with many people I have had contact with. The neglect of self is so common that we typically do not even notice. We tend to forget our likes, dislikes, weaknesses, and strengths, things that give us pleasure, hobbies, and the activities we are good at.

We have lost things we loved to do; although they might not get us close to our materialistic goals, they will undoubtedly keep us happy and keep us engaged, which is important in our lives. When they are not there, they can cause other things like emotional imbalance that can lead to mental illness like depression, etc. Since health is essential, we seek ways and means to manage the mental illness, and we seek medical attention or external help to cure it.

Meditation is also one of the ways or means of managing loneliness. It is advisable to include meditation in your daily routine, irrespective of if you feel lonely or not; make it a part of your regular life.

You need to focus on yourself. If you have managed and understand yourself as a person and understand that there will be times you will be alone, you will find ways to manage loneliness. This is because you know it will come, as you have been dealing with it every day from childhood to your present day. However, somehow, if in your adult life, you feel you cannot manage it anymore, this is because you have completely forgotten yourself.

I have seen top managers who manage big firms but are big failures because they cannot manage themselves well. It is imperative that as we grow and become managers or grow our businesses, we learn how to manage and take care of ourselves. I know that many of us want to attain a managing director's position in life, but executive positions or designations will not always remain with us. It will only stay with us as long as we are in this materialistic world; what will stay with you till the end is you, yourself.

The remedy to loneliness lies in managing yourself and following a routine that keeps you physically and mentally healthy and active. You should manage your daily work and find ways to address loneliness by engaging your mind in interest-based activities. Play a game of your choice which keeps you engaged. Remember your core strengths and be sure to capitalize on them (like the way I have done by capturing my thoughts in the form of this book, despite being physically alone and mentally lonely). In the same way, we go to a gym to keep our bodies healthy, we should do meditation and yoga regularly to keep our minds focused, calm, and healthy.

We have engrossed ourselves in this materialistic world so much that we have entirely forgotten ourselves; we only live for others, whereas managing ourselves is the most crucial thing in life. Find out your strengths, write out those things, materialistic or non-materialistic things that will give you happiness, note them somewhere or keep them in mind. And when that period of loneliness that I mentioned at the beginning of the chapter rears its ugly head, which is bound to happen to everyone, use those things that make you happy to occupy yourself. You will not feel so lonely again.

Engage yourself in any sport and play regularly; it will keep you mentally and physically active. Meet and make new friends with like minds, have fun, get a new hobby, put yourself in a great state of mind, engage in those things that make you happy, and not feel lonely.

Most of us are ready with our retirement plans and know the source of funds for retirement. Do we have a similar strategy to manage our loneliness post-retirement? I have my doubts. We are not prepared to handle our loneliness when we are no longer working, retire, or become obsolete at work and leave life's stardom. Nobody plans to address loneliness during that time.

It is essential to stay positive in life no matter the situation. No situation in life lasts forever, so always stay positive and know that whether the condition is good or bad, it is not permanent, the same with loneliness. Note that when you are positive, when you are working on your strength, and you know yourself better, you will never find yourself alone.

I am in that stage of living alone as I am thousands of kilometers away from my family, but I recalled my strength of doing something new and always pulling something out of the box. I remembered my writing strength as I love to do out of box activities to add value to people's lives. It began as a hobby for me while I was working in India, to write things down in the form of journaling or presentations to add value to people's lives. When I was with my previous job, after business reviews, I used to make small presentations, two to three slides around 'living well' that could add value to people. I am not an expert in coaching, but I used my life experiences to communicate with my team. As my colleagues used to reach out to me concerning the presentations, judging by their responses, I can say it was good, and it boosts my morale, building my confidence.

Though I am not an excellent writer, I knew about this strength, and this made me handle my loneliness in Nigeria as I put my energy into writing all this. Eventually, after almost a year, those small write-ups that formed presentations are now going into a book.

All I am saying is, know your strength whether you are with family or staying alone. Those strengths will always give you confidence throughout your life and will not allow you to feel lonely; they will engage you, motivate you and make you feel happy, which is very important in life.

Loneliness is experienced when we miss someone or our life's great moments. We should preserve those moments in the form of a soft or hard copy. It will help us manage loneliness when it comes. Also, we live our lives and follow our routines, which mostly have only our professional time table, we can incorporate a timetable with professional and personal practices. We can continue the personal habits when we retire, remain busy, occupied, and we will not feel lonely at the later part of our life.

"Life is like an open book exam; choose your answers wisely" - Rajeev Dua

Chapter 24

Life is like an open book exam

Life is like an exam; your answers are being judged at every level. The difference between the normal exam and the life exam is that you are given a particular timeline, specific course, and study materials relevant to the examination during the routine exam, and you are pretty sure of the course you are writing. On the other hand, life is like an open book exam with no specific textbook to read. You can be asked any question without prior intimation, unlike your standard college or school exams.

When appearing for a regular exam, you are mostly not allowed to carry your textbooks, whereas you are allowed to carry as many books as you can in the life exam. Some people refer to textbooks, motivational books, and some guidance from consultants, seniors, mentors, and some attend spiritual or intellectual seminars to appear for the life exam. Yet, you can still fail.

When taking normal exams, the answers to the questions are always the same for all the participants, whereas, in the life exam, solutions to the same problem will always vary from person to person. The life answers will differ depending on the person, circumstances, situation, and understanding of life. There is nothing like a wrong or right answer in life exams; no one will ask you the source of your answers. Life exams should be attended wisely and with one fundamental thing, which is COMMON SENSE.

If you appear for your life exam intelligently, and with common sense, I can guarantee that you will pass it with full distinction. Unfortunately, common sense is something that is not so common these days.

In normal exams, your answer sheet gets judged by one of your lecturers or teachers. Still, in your life exam, the answer sheet is checked by many judges like friends, family, colleagues, neighbors and customers, amongst others, including yourself. So, no matter how many books you refer to while appearing in your life exam, you cannot satisfy all the people checking your answer sheets. The best way to appear for your life exams is to stay real, humble, and use your common sense.

While it is important to look at the marks secured in your life exam as given by your friends, relatives, colleagues, and others, bear in mind that you cannot satisfy everyone, even though you have respect for their opinions and suggestions. Note that what is essential is to self-evaluate your own answers to your life exam because no one can judge your answers to life except YOU.

Life can throw some questions or challenges at you which might not be relevant to you, and it leaves you with the option of ignoring them completely. Sometimes, ignoring some life questions is the best answer to it; we do not need to attempt some questions if you ask me. We cannot participate in and win all the challenges in our lives. However, some situations force us to try several questions of life that are not so relevant to us; we then make efforts to find answers to them. These are those questions that, if not attempted wisely, force us to forget our own identity, distract us from our purpose in life and our core strengths.

For example - buying a car that is better than your neighbor's, having better jewelry than one of your friends, wearing a better brand as compared to your colleague, or going out to a weekly dinner with friends to increase your social status and enjoying an international vacation every year, similar to one of your relatives. These are a few of the questions, which in my opinion, you do not need to attempt unless you are sure of your capabilities and your own strengths. If you try such questions without adequate preparation, then chances are you will be successful for a short while but ultimately be at a loss in the long run. It is not necessary to attempt all the questions answered by your friends, relatives, and colleagues, just for the sake of trying them without your proper preparation.

So, always understand the situation, take your time, evaluate your capability, look at the resources available to you and apply common sense. You will be able to solve your life's questions, and this will make you successful in your professional and personal life.

There is always a right time to attempt some challenges or questions of life; one should have the presence of mind to judge that time right. Some solutions or answers might not be relevant today but will surely be relevant tomorrow. For example, if I had attempted to launch an e-commerce store thirty years ago, people would have seen me as a fool because internet penetration and online buying was not so widespread during those days. Now, however, we buy most of our goods online, so launching a social media campaign or a product to be sold only through an online channel can be considered today, something which seemed impossible thirty years ago. So always look for the right time to attempt specific questions of life.

There is no harm in attempting some questions you do not know the answers to, called risk-taking. However, trying them regularly, without proper preparation, without evaluating your own strengths, or even without developing your capabilities, is something I do not encourage. If you want to take a risk in life, ensure that you prepare for it. Enhance your skills and abilities, do not take those questions or challenges just for the sake of it; if you are not ready, the chances are that you will fail in those exams and the result of failing over and over again is that you forget your strengths, and capabilities. This is because you are trying to copy someone else and are not leaning on your own strengths.

Think of it as a race track where you keep meeting a roadblock. Instead of turning back and attempting another road, you stay put and keep ramming the wall, hoping that the roadblock will automatically disappear. You feel some things are very important in life and believe you need to get the answers to them, and when you do not, you keep attempting it. When you keep getting the wrong answers, you move from the right track to the wrong track, you self-destruct, and at the end of the day, you blame yourself.

We need to understand that not every situation has an immediate solution. You need to apply common sense in such cases. Common sense is thinking rationally about things that give practical solutions to problems. If you think rational and keep your emotions aside, you will be able to provide genuine solutions to your problems, and you would not necessarily answer all the questions that come your way. Attempting life's situation and giving a wrong answer gives your life a wrong direction, and that is why it is better to prepare for situations, leave emotions aside, have a fall-back option and be realistic, with your studies, profession, business, personal life, and parenthood, amongst other life situations.

Every day, everyone learns. Learning is something that never ends, learning is unending. If you have a learning attitude, you will not fail in life and will have answers to all questions and situations you confront. Learning can happen with your teachers, superiors, mentors, juniors and even with your kids. It can happen from anywhere and with anyone irrespective of age, course or trade. We learn from non-living things also; we even learn from nature as mentioned in the previous chapter.

We go to several motivational speakers, coaches, and mentors to find solutions to problems in life. Still, life is not like a textbook where there is a particular answer to a question because life's situation varies from person to person and the answer also varies. There is no harm in listening to the motivational speakers or having a mentor as this adds value to your life. This is how you can keep that learning attitude alive in your life.

Have that learning attitude in mind, have common sense in mind, and have a practical approach in mind; you will not get into uncomfortable situations, and you will not attempt questions based on how someone else tried it. You will not think that if so and so have a big house, a large car, a large bank account and comfortable life, so should I.

So, do not copy answers given by other people in life because their answers will differ as their situations are different from yours. Live your life based on your own strengths, your own capabilities, your own learnings, and do not copy. This is because when you copy and follow someone else's path, you lose your core identity, your core strength and that someone else path will not take you to your destination. Copying sometimes is not very bad, provided you are adding value to what is being copied and that path is taking you towards your own goal.

Life will give you challenges, and it will also make available the answer all around you. It is left to you to provide the right or wrong answer: choose your answers wisely and not copy the answers given by others. That is the mistake most of us make, and we later fail in the examination called "Life."

"While appearing for a normal exam, different individuals will have same answer to a particular question, whereas in life's exam, the answer to a question will vary for each individual" – Rajeev Dua

"Realizing that you are lost in the
journey called life is the biggest step
towards finding yourself" - Rajeev Dua

Chapter 25

Find yourself again

If someone very close to us goes missing, we would quite likely be sad and worried, and then we would start thinking and looking for ways to get him or her back. We would either try searching in places where we may have left them, and if we do not find them, we would speak to our common acquaintances to check if they know the missing person's whereabouts. If there is still no result, we would then go to the police and make a report. The police will gather all kinds of required information from us regarding the person to find him or her.

If you go to the police station to lodge a complaint about a missing person, the first thing the police will ask you for is the person's identity. Details like the name, appearance, and identification marks amongst other information; you will then try and recap all the information regarding the person to give it to them to make it easy for the police to find the person. Without the information on identification marks, name, image, and appearance, the police will find it challenging to identify the missing person.

What if you tell the police that you are looking for your own self and start describing yourself to them, telling them that you were last found or seen at such a place, therefore you would like to find yourself. Do you not think the police will probably look at you funny? They will be asking you this question repeatedly, 'Are you sure you are looking for yourself? Are you sure you are lost because you are describing yourself and sitting here, in front of me? The policeman will definitely have a good laugh, invite other colleagues to witness the meeting, who will also have a good laugh, and tell you that you cannot be lost when everyone can see and can hear you speak. They will think you are going insane.

To find yourself is the same process as finding someone else. The only difference is that you will not be narrating it to anyone but yourself, because no one else can find the inner you (your soul) except you. To find yourself, you will not be narrating your physical attributes to yourself, but you will describe your own strengths, your interests, happy moments, childhood friends, favorite places, favourite food, etc.

In the journey called life, we have lost who we are, our strengths, likes, and dislikes. We have lost those happy moments that used to give us pleasure. We have made ourselves so ordinary that we do not care for ourselves anymore. Instead, we have started living life for society, friends, a job, a business, our bosses, neighbours, and competition. We are chasing unrealistic goals, while playing so many roles simultaneously, and as such, we have lost our own identities. We have kept ourselves aside and started living an artificial life to please others. However, the good news is that we can still find ourselves again.

It is difficult, though, to find yourself if you do not know who you are. You can know your face, your height, how you look, and how you dress based on what the mirror shows, but not know your soul. It can be challenging to know who you are amidst the many associations you have kept over time and the several roles you have played.

Finding yourself is more than knowing how you look; it is to understand who you are and your role in life so far. It is to determine those places, situations, and circumstances where you might have lost yourself. This is essential so that you can go back to those situations, go back to those places, travel back to those years and try to find yourself again.

Most of us do not even get to discover that we have lost our own selves in the journey called life and we only get to know this at the later stages of our lives, and by that time it is too late. We get engrossed in the materialistic world such that we do not focus and pamper ourselves anymore. Our family goals become different from ours, and as a result, the ecosystem around them does not have a place for us to fit in to. Similarly, the ecosystem around us does not allow our family members to fit in. We are all moving in different directions without letting each other know about our respective goals and desires; thus, we do not empathize with each other; instead, we get judgmental. Though it is vital to have our personal goals and chase after them, we are human, and we live with family. It is equally important that our families align with our goals and we are in line with theirs. There might be different opinions amongst the family regarding the respective goals, still, it is always better to find common ground and move in the same direction.

We falsely assume that we are all moving in one direction, whereas the fact is that we are all moving in different directions. We look for perfection in the roles we play, and as a result, we have forgotten our own selves. It is essential to keep our family members aware of our strengths, dreams and desires; we should also know theirs to move in one direction as a family and fulfill our individual and family goals together. There is no point in achieving personal goals at the cost of our own happiness and that of our families.

You should be proactive in finding yourself back because it is a fact that you will get lost in the journey called life, so it is better to be proactive. Along with playing so many roles in life, you should continue with your childhood hobbies, live your life on your own strengths, and continue playing your favourite sport as this will help distract you from the stressors of life. Make sure to visit those places you like to be the most; keep your childhood friends close by. Do not lose contact with them irrespective of their social status. Continue with your favourite food, remember all your likes and dislikes; all these will help keep you alive while playing your many roles in this materialistic world.

It is also worth noting that in the journey of life, you will have good times and bad times. If you always have good times, you will not have value for the good times, and if you always have bad times, you will not enjoy what life is. So note, life is full of challenges, but when you have those bad times, you should remember your core strengths and understand how to use them to overcome those challenges. Most times, you get so deep into the challenges that you forget your strengths and then give up your life to the challenges. That is so wrong! You must learn how to manage challenges using your strengths as a weapon.

For example, when I came here to Nigeria, I was all alone. I am a very social person, and it was difficult for me to cope with my loneliness. There was a point when loneliness started to get to me; I would just break down and cry, but despite the tears, I would take selfies to remember my tough times. Though I was in tears, I was not weak; I was determined. I remembered my strength of writing, capitalized on it, and survived on it. I used my writing skills to manage my loneliness. This book is the result of my determination to not give in to loneliness.

Make yourself special, do not make yourself out as an ordinary person in front of your own self. Please remember, you are the most valuable and important person to you. It might sound selfish, but you will not be able to make others happy without being happy yourself. So focus, pamper yourself, and play on your strengths while walking the path of happiness. It will take you to your desired destination of making you and others happy too.

Now that you have read this book and have found yourself to be your best friend, keep visiting places you love, eat the food you like (as far it does not affect your health), keep hangouts with childhood friends, and do those hobbies which bring you happiness. Ensure that you develop a mechanism to remember these activities often while playing your different roles in this journey called life; they will keep you alive and will not allow you to lose yourself.

Epilogue by -
Doc Harbhajan Batth

The book "The Lost You" provides readers with a tidy guide to a thrilling and twisting life full of self-discovery. This book will serve as a treat to readers who may be stuck with life's burdens, as well as a reassurance that self-discovery is possible and not in vain when ventured. It is a journey of life, springing new wonders all the time.

The first time I met Rajeev was at the domestic airport in Port Harcourt, Nigeria. We were waiting for the same flight, which was experiencing some delay. A couple of other Indian nationals were waiting for the Lagos bound flight, but somehow, I felt positive vibes from Rajeev, sitting two seats away from me in the departure hall. After exchanging glances and nods of appreciation, we started a conversation.

It was fascinating getting to know this young, handsome lady killer, who was highly informed and had a versatile personality. Since we had lots of time, after exchanging pleasantries, our discussion went to Nigeria's social, economic, political, and business landscape, a topic I always cherish as Nigeria is my Karmabhoomi (land of actions).

I was impressed with Rajeev's knowledge of the subjects even though he was a JJC (Johnny Just Come – Nigerian idiom for a newcomer) in Nigeria.

Around that time, I was writing my first book, - "Fixing Stereotypes.... My Way", so I took the courage to ask him for his opinion. To my surprise, many of his thoughts were similar to mine. There was an instant bond between us; as it is said, "birds of a feather flock together."

At our first meeting, our discussion mainly focused on self-growth, personal development, skills upgrade, and my published books, at which he expressed the desire to publish his own book. Lo! Here comes his first book - 'THE LOST YOU.'

After reading Rajeev's book, one may ask, how can you play all such roles simultaneously and excel in all?

Depending on that answer, which only you can give, you either stay on the path or adjust towards the right direction; that is how you self-introspect. However, the trick may indeed lie in one's degree of E.Q (i.e., emotional quotient) or empathy.

I practically love the chapter on nature, so as you read, be like a tree, grow strong roots, adapt to some strong values and live by them. Discard dead leaves (unhealthy competition), grow strong branches, and never become one with the wind (people's opinion).

For Rajeev, the key to being a good human lies in these three treasures - compassion, moderation, and lastly, humility. These three things are all that is necessary to point one's moral compass in the right direction.

Are you hoping to read a sequel? Readers must be immersed in the next chapter of this saga if he plans to do that! Accolades to the accuracy of Rajeev's ideas.

'Shall I compare thee to a summer's day? Thou art more lovely and more temperate.'

(Sonnet 18 – William Shakespeare)

By Dr. Batth Harbahajan

स्वयं से गुफ्तगू

ज़िन्दगी की दौड़ मे ओहदे बहुत मिले, ओहदों की चाँदनी से जब हटी नज़र !
पैसा बहुत दिखा मगर आये ना तुम नज़र, कैसी काम की यह डगर !!

पैसे की दौड़ ने बनाया मुझ को मदहोश !
तू जाग कर भी मेरे दोस्त क्यों है बेहोश !!

इस बेहोशी से जग जा, और जला ले अपनी ज़िंदगी का दिया !
यह तू ही है, हाँ तू ही तो है, जो सब के लिए जिया !!

अब जल्दी से उठ जा, और ज़रा अपने बारे मे सोच !
और ज़िन्दगी के पैरों से तू निकाल दे यह मोच !!

चल वापस चलें उस डगर पर, जहाँ से करी थी शुरुआत !
और दौड़ के करते हैं अपने स्वयं से मुलाकात !!

मुलाकात करके करते है, चल खुद से गुफ्तगू !
कुछ थाम लेते हैं, अपनी ख्वाईशो की जुस्तजू !!

In The End...

When we started our professional life
It appeared to be as good as a newly wedded wife

The way a newly wedded bride gradually becomes fat
We also became arrogant and brat

We put on a lot of weight of money and positions
We judge people only based on their limitations

Limitations are part and parcel of every human being
Still, we judge others as if we don't have any such thing

Please leave your arrogance and remember your early professional days
As every individual had innocence which got lost in some old dark bays

An employer can become an employee, and vice a versa
Your paisa can work as rupee and your rupee as paisa

This is a game of positions and posts
Focus on your learning and don't become a professional ghost

One day when you look back, it will look like a dream
You will be left with just thin milk, with no butter or cream

Stay on Earth and be humble
Because WE all one day shall roll like a bundle.

www.ingramcontent.com/pod-product-compliance
Lightning Source LLC
Chambersburg PA
CBHW030308160726
47992CB00005B/1925